Egg Cures

Proven Recipes and Techniques

Scott Haugen

Frank Amato
PORTLAND

Acknowledgments

J would like to thank all of the people mentioned in the pages that follow, for offering their time, advice, and, most of all, their coveted egg-curing recipes. Without your willingness to share, this book would not have come to fruition.

In my research for this book, I learned many things. Some folks were eager to share their cures, others took a little prodding, while still others would rather give up their boats and homes before divulging their secret recipes.

For those of you who did share your egg-curing secrets, you should be proud. Today, more than ever, sportsmen need to be a cohesive unit, and this means doing whatever it takes to get people on the rivers, in the hills, and along the marshes. Though the days where we head to our favorite streams for peace, tranquility, and yes, fishing, may be gone we musn't forget that every angler yearns for that special moment. In a sense, we are all intruders, but we lust for the same experiences as can only be offered through the outdoors.

By being stellar sportsmen, abiding by all game regulations, and being as positive as we can about the sportfishing industry, together we can ensure a promising future for the sport we all love. After all, any of us would agree we want our children and grandchildren to experience fishing as we have been lucky enough to know it. Through our perseverance and dedication, they can.

It is my hope that everyone who reads this book will try at least a few of these egg-curing recipes on their favorite streams. It is also my wish that each and every one of us passes some of this valuable information along to other anglers – including novices. By introducing newcomers to the sport, not only do you promote one of the greatest pastimes known to man, but you help bring valued money into the economy and management programs, something we will be more dependent upon to help preserve sport fisheries in coming years.

Happy Casting!

Scott Haugen

© 2002 Scott Haugen

Published in 2002 by
Frank Amato Publications, Inc.
PO Box 82112 • Portland, Oregon 97282 • (503) 653-8108
Softbound ISBN: 1-57188-238-3 • Softbound UPC: 0-66066-00492-5
Photography by Scott Haugen
Book Design: Esther Poleo
Printed in Hong Kong

Contents

Introduction

As an outdoor writer, nothing is more gratifying than meeting someone who has read my work and comes away with something new and enlightening they can apply to their own fishing. As a sportsman I feel the same way. If there is any way I can help someone ethically catch more fish, live new experiences, and learn new techniques, I'll do it.

Having spent over a decade in the field of education, perhaps it's my nature as a teacher to offer advice to anglers intent on learning something new. That may explain why I find sharing information so gratifying. Perhaps it's because I've observed my father doing the same thing for the past 35 years, enhancing the lives of many anglers along the way.

My father, too, was a teacher and coach and it has always been his nature to share information anytime anyone asked. He carries no secrets.

I learn something new about fishing every day I'm out, even on days I don't catch fish. I'm always searching for new tactics or effective approaches that have worked for other anglers over generations. I also enjoy discovering new approaches on my own. To those people willing to share such information, you deserve a pat on the back; I commend you for doing your part to enhance our sport.

Why A Book on Egg Cures?

Of all the methods anglers can employ to catch salmon and steelhead, using natural bait is the most widespread. Of the natural baits, roe, or eggs, is considered by many to be the best. This unique book is, to my knowledge, the first written solely dedicated to egg cures. By sharing the new information within these pages, it is my hope that more anglers will take to the river, catch more fish, and experience, first hand, what it is that makes fishing for salmon and steelhead so addicting.

No matter where you live, these cures can be used in any streams open to bait fishing. If you live east of the mountain states and are eager to learn more about cluster and single-egg cures, this book will set you on your way. If you're from the Pacific Northwest, intent on picking up recipes to be used on single eggs that can be fished in roe bags, keep turning the pages. From Alaska, through Canada, down to California, and across to the Great Lakes drainages, the cures in this book can be put to the test. Egg cures know no geographic or political boundaries.

The egg cures shared in this book come from five states and two Canadian provinces. They were selected from a wide range of recipes–some simple, some complex. For every cure that appears in print, three others were considered for inclusion. The ingredients and handling processes were carefully chosen to include diverse yet comprehensive information useful to any angler wishing to try out the cures in this book. There are also words of wisdom from people who have devoted their lives and careers to fishing egg cures.

These recipes and techniques come from anglers who catch fish. These guys have been in the trenches for years, some for several decades. Not all of them are guides; it's not that they couldn't be, it's that they chose other professions, cherishing fishing as a preferred hobby.

For various reasons, several guides I approached were reluctant to share their egg-curing recipes. Either they didn't want to divulge their secrets, got their recipes from fellow guides who swore them to secrecy, or felt they were on a good thing they didn't want to let go just yet. To some extent I can appreciate that, but some went to extremes.

"A book on this subject won't be worth a darn," remarked a noted Pacific Northwest guide. "Any guide who has a cure that works won't tell you, and anyone who does tell you, doesn't have a cure worth printing." With that, he bid me goodbye and hung up. He wouldn't so much as spend a few minutes sharing the handling process of his eggs.

Another popular guide remarked, "I do this for a living and am not about to share any of what I do, otherwise people wouldn't book with me."

I did run across eager guides, and several avid anglers, willing to share what they know about eggs and cures. These gentlemen have the foresight to carry our sport into the 21st century by doing what they can to involve as many anglers as possible in our sport, and for that we are all grateful. The wisdom passed along in these pages is immeasurable, and the numbers of fish that have succumbed to these fishermen would boggle the mind.

What I did learn from the dozens of guides I talked with is that due to time constraints, many are utilizing prepackaged cures for the simple reason that they're quick, easy, and effective. After long days on the river, day after day, it's easy to understand why they move to cures harboring simple procedures.

The majority of cures in this book come from veterans of the sport — guys who have time to experiment with cures and study, in detail, the effects of different chemicals in brines and dry cures. In these pages you will find 27 egg-curing recipes provided by 20 different anglers. But when you start experimenting with the scents and oils mentioned by these men, hundreds of variations are unveiled. Each entry includes one or two recipes and/or details relating to egg cures with step-by-step procedures that will take you from start to finish in the curing process. Some of the people who shared these cures have theories and strategies on the curing process that they are faithful to, things they have learned over years of trial and error. Others are constantly experimenting, never content with their end product.

It is my hope that you not only enjoy this book, but find it highly educational. The ultimate goal is that it serves as a catalyst for anglers to catch more fish. I look forward to the day we cross paths on the river. Just maybe you'll have a new cure you'd like to share.

Egg Preparation

Before getting into the recipes, tips, and detailed information, let's first look at the most important step: working with quality eggs. A fresh, high-quality salmon or steelhead egg is vital to obtaining a good cure. In most, if not all, of the cures in this book, eggs comprise over 90% of the ingredients. No matter how special your cure, or how well you've perfected the operation, it means nothing if you start with poor-quality eggs.

A high-quality skein of eggs is odorless and free of blood. It's vital to cure your eggs as soon as possible, before they turn color, lose moisture, or develop a foul odor. Even under the most ideal of circumstances, each minute after a fish dies, the eggs inside her drop in quality. To help promote fresh, high-quality eggs, you can do two things: bleed the fish or remove the eggs completely.

After killing the hen, inserting a long knife into the underside of the upper belly, at the heart, is effective for releasing blood. Be sure the blade enters in front of the pectoral fins so as to avoid damaging the eggs. This is where most of the blood coagulates in a dead fish, and much of it congeals around the eggs. Cutting the gills is perhaps the most common method of releasing blood, while slicing the base of the underside of the tail is also effective. Releasing blood ensures your eggs

Raw, freezer-burned eggs (left) will not yield good bait, no matter what cure is applied. Fresh eggs (right) are what you must start with.

This fish was not bled after being caught. Be certain excess blood is removed from any skein prior to curing.

Properly removing eggs is a vital, often overlooked, step in obtaining quality eggs. Cut sha-low and lift up on the belly to protect against damaging the skein.

will not change color, and will remain odor-free and maintain a healthy appearance.

Removing your eggs from the fish is also an option. On several occasions I've removed skeins from hens, minutes after being caught. Done immediately after dispatching the fish, eggs are blood-free and gorgeous in color. I place them in a clean baggie to ensure they don't come in contact with other contaminants, then place them on ice, where they can be kept cool. As soon as I get home, they go to the cure jar. I always keep a premixed jar of my powdered cure ready to go, so I can get the eggs in it immediately.

Washington guide, Bruce Gipple, advised that when going after ocean fish, removing their eggs within

Starting with a fresh skein of eggs is best for maximizing the cures you work with.

The quicker the eggs are removed from fish, the less likely bacteria are to infect the skeins, the better quality your cured eggs will turn out.

five minutes of being caught is critical. His reasoning makes sense: Salmon in the ocean are still actively feeding. When killed, the bacterial byproducts in their gut are oftentimes regurgitated. These acids and bacteria can escape into the fish's body cavity, tainting the eggs. This is why Gipple bleeds his ocean fish immediately, then removes the eggs five minutes later.

When thawing frozen eggs to cure, do it slowly, to help prevent the cells from softening any further.

No matter where in the process you handle your eggs, wearing rubber gloves is a good idea. Remember, a fish's sense of smell is measured in parts per billion, and human odors released from oils through our skin can make a difference in egg smell. I know of several guides and anglers who catch impressive numbers of fish each year, that never touch the eggs with bare hands, from the time they are removed from the fish to the time they go on the hook.

Finally, you may want to watch the foods you eat when fishing with eggs. I've fished with guys in Alaska who would not allow a person in the boat until they got rid of the banana in their lunch sack. Some guides strongly advise against their clients even eating bananas at breakfast, or anytime prior to hitting the river. Potassium, found in bananas, is reported to put off a scent that will drive fish away. I spoke with one guide who even tried placing drops of potassium in an aquarium to observe the fish behaviors. The fish scattered every direction. He's now a believer in the no-potassium rule.

Rubber boots are also a good idea when fishing with eggs. Odors are not as easily transferred on rubber, so when your baited hook sits in the bottom of the boat – where you just stepped – the chance of your eggs becoming contaminated greatly diminishes if rubber boots are worn.

It may seem a bit on the fanatical side, but attention to detail is what many anglers credit for their success. In combination, several minute technicalities add up to a major role in your egg-cure performance. Throughout this book, fishermen offer further advice on techniques for handling eggs.

The Final Product

The ultimate goal of most egg cures is to harbor a scent and visually attractive color that will maintain over extended periods to entice fish to bite. The longer a scent takes to drain, or milk out from an egg, the better the odds of a fish finding it.

Plasmolysis is the technical term whereby the protoplasm contracts away from the cell wall due to the withdrawal of liquid by osmosis when the cell is in a liquid of greater solute density than what's in the cell itself. In simpler terms, when a cured egg enters water, the contents move from the egg, through the semipermiable membrane of the cell wall, and into the river. It's these scents and visual stimuli we strive to make last as long as possible to increase the chance of a fish locating our bait.

The longer it takes for plasmolysis, or milking, to be carried out, the longer a bait can be fished. The longer a bait can be fished, the more time is spent with terminal gear in the water and the higher your odds of catching fish.

Mind you, fish won't react to the same attractant every time, so don't limit yourself to one cure. We've all been in situations where we fished a hole and were convinced nothing was there, only to pull out, have another angler step in and nail fish. The fish were likely there the whole time and the conditions above and below water remained constant. The only difference, the bait changed.

Maybe you presented a sulfite-based cure while the angler behind you tried a borax-based cure. Perhaps you tried shrimp oil while the other person introduced anise. Had you carried a variety of cures, chances are those fish would have been yours.

If you're searching for the perfect cure, you may find what you consider to be just that in this book. But don't stop there. Sure I have my favorite cure, as do most guys, but I don't know of one angler who has constant success with one cure every time they hit the river.

Broaden your spectrum. Find two, three, or four cures that you consider worthy of constant use. By arming yourself with a variety of cures – be they different ratios of key ingredients, dry versus wet cures, dyed or natural colors – you will find an egg with which you are confident. If fishing a hole and your favorite cure doesn't work, don't hesitate to switch to another, or even a third.

Open your mind, pay attention to details, and put forth the effort. By doing so, you will catch fish.

A final note: There are many guides and manufacturers mentioned in this book. To obtain their contact information, refer to the appendix on page 103.

Experimenting with multiple cures can increase your success on the river.

A rich, deep-colored bait, cured and ready to go. This is the end result many anglers strive for.

The Author's Favorite Cure

INGREDIENTS
- 1 1/2 cups borax
- 3/4 cup white sugar
- 1 tablespoon sodium bisulfite
- 6-10 drops pure anise oil

Of the hundreds of feature articles I've written for magazines around the world, none has received more feedback than the article that appeared in the April-May 2001 issue of Salmon Trout Steelheader magazine. The article was titled "A Proven Cure" and to this day I bump into anglers on the river, at local tackle shops, and at sportsmen's shows who read that piece. Many tell me their success on salmon and steelhead has increased due to this cure. Some claim it has given them new hope when pursing these fine fish.

This recipe has been in my family for three generations, and I've been told it's one of the most sought-after recipes in the fishing world. An Indian gentleman from the Umpqua Basin shared it with my grandfather and a friend of his, and it's been catching fish ever since.

Dad and I use this cure most of the time, on spring and fall chinook, silver salmon, and winter and summer steelhead. We've also used it successfully on chum and red salmon. We've fished it in rivers throughout the West, from California up to British Columbia and Alaska.

The recipe is simple, especially if you think of it from a scientific standpoint. The objective in attaining a realistic bait is that it looks real, contains odors attractive to anadromous fish, and holds up after repeated use.

Only four ingredients are needed: Borax, white sugar, sodium bisulfite, and anise oil.

Borax and white sugar can be bought at nearly any supermarket. Sodium bisulfite (NaS_3) is available from your local pharmacy while anise oil can be obtained from a scientific supply company.

When purchasing the sodium bisulfite, be sure to get the purified (often called reagent) grade. There is a cheaper, "food grade" but avoid the urge to pick it up, it's just not as effective. The same holds true for the anise oil; there are a few choices, buy only the "pure grade" which is FCC approved.

Borax draws the moisture out of the eggs. The more borax you use, the drier the cure. Sugar serves as a hardener, toughening up the skein and ultimately keeping your bait intact and therefore on the hook longer.

Sodium bisulfite is a color preservative, locking in the natural color of the eggs you are curing. I like it because it's clean, odorless, and stain-free when working with it. If the color of the eggs you are curing don't appeal to you, there are other options.

The author's favorite cure is one of the most sought after in the egg curing world. Having the proper ingredients is key.

Specialty packaged cures, such as Pro-Cure, can be added to give your eggs the desired color. We've used these products with good success, but frankly, I get tired of the gooey mess and stained clothes.

Jell-O also works if you are looking to add color. Darken your eggs by adding powdered Jell-O. Raspberry is a favorite and mixes well with the sodium bisulfite. If you want even more color in the eggs, simply add more Jell-O, allowing time for it to soak through the semipermiable membrane of each egg, and thus locking color inside the cells. The more Jell-O powder you add, the darker the eggs will turn. The anise oil masks the raspberry flavor.

As for the anise oil – if there were a secret, this is it – the key is to purchase the real thing. I've never smelled a commercially produced anise oil I liked; they're too diluted and do not stay with the eggs long. Pure anise oil is potent, less than a dozen drops are needed for each curing. The 500-milliliter container it comes in will last several seasons.

Procedure

Start by cutting your eggs. This is a crucial step, for if done improperly, the eggs won't stay on your hook. Take the skein in hand and cut it lengthwise, ensuring to keep as much skein intact as possible. For large skeins you may end up with 3-4 long strips. Next, cut across the long strips, into your desired sizes, making sure ample skein is on every single bait. If you don't have plenty of skein, the baits won't snug up in your egg loop and you'll be wasting time on the water.

The size of container you use for curing your eggs depends on the amount you'll be curing. If it's the eggs of one summer steelhead, a small jar will suffice. If its a bucket full of salmon eggs, you'll need several large jars. Whatever size you use make it glass or clear plastic, something you can see through.

Mix the powdered ingredients in a separate container from that which you'll be curing the eggs in. Blend 1 1/2 cups borax, 3/4 cup white sugar and one tablespoon sodium bisulfite. If you desire darker eggs, Jell-O can now be mixed in. Anise oil will be added later. Break up the borax so no chunks remain and thoroughly mix the powders.

Sprinkle an inch layer of the powder mixture into the bottom of the curing jar. You want a heavy layer of powder on the bottom to soak up juices that precipitate from above.

Next, place a layer of precut eggs over the bottom layer of powder mixture. Add 2-3 drops of anise oil atop the eggs and cover with a layer of powder mixture so no eggs can be seen when looking into the mouth of the jar. Repeat the whole process until all of your baits are in the jar. The top and final layer is another heavy coating of the powder mixture. Tomorrow this will become the bottom of the curing jar.

All layers complete, be sure the lid is securely fastened.

Tending the Mixture

Place the jar upright in a dry, cool place (or at least room temperature). A dark corner of the garage or pumphouse works well. An important factor is keeping sunlight from reaching the jar. Any sunlight penetrating the jar sets off a chemical reaction that will darken the eggs, turning them nearly black and therefore worthless. I learned this the hard way.

Let the jar set for 24 hours or so, then turn it over. Do not shake the jar, just flip it on its lid. The key is to have the juices seep slowly to the bottom, carrying scent and color

Rotating the eggs to allow juices to precipitate through the baits is an important step in this cure.

into the cells. Let set another day, then flip the jar back on its bottom. After the third day, the eggs are prime and ready to go.

If you're doing a lot of fishing, you can use the eggs after one day. We've done this many times, it's just that the eggs aren't as tough as they could be. If you can leave the cure setting three full days the eggs will be hardier, holding in your egg loop longer.

After day three, I prefer air-drying the eggs. This can be done by placing the entire contents of the jar on white paper towels or some type of drying rack. Plastic flats from a plant nursery also work well. The woven plastic holds the eggs yet provide gaps to allow air to come in from all sides, drying the eggs evenly.

If you dry your eggs on unscented paper towels, flip them over once their surface has dried to the desired texture. A second, fresh layer of towels may be needed. Be sure the drying is done in a shaded area.

How long you air-dry the eggs depends on what your objective is and also weather conditions. On hot, dry summer days, 15 minutes may suffice. On moist, cool winter days, it may take several hours. If you can situate the eggs so that a breeze whisks by, say under a patio or carport, this process will be expedited.

If you want hard baits, let them dry until they reach desired firmness. If you want soft eggs, don't leave them out very long. If it's wet baits you want, you may not air-dry them at all. Avoid letting the eggs get too dry, when cinched against the shank of the hook in your egg loop they could be sliced in two.

Storage

Place the finished eggs in a Ziploc® bag and add a couple more drops of anise oil. Shake the bag to disperse the oil and store in the refrigerator – preferably not the family refrigerator as the smell of pure anise oil can be overpowering. If you're not going to use them for a few weeks, stow them in the freezer.

We have kept cured eggs in the freezer up to a year and they performed flawlessly. If you are storing them for a greater length of time – or if your freezer seems to accumulate too much moisture – you are in jeopardy of freezer burn. To retard freezer burn, store the eggs in vacuum packed bags. Or, you can add straight borax to a bag or plastic container full of eggs. The borax will soak up the moisture that condenses in the freezer, saving most of the eggs from burning. The outer layer of eggs may turn hard and yellow, but inside, the eggs should be in good shape.

Which eggs work best?

This cure has been used extensively on West Coast salmon and steelhead eggs. I even caught steelhead on shad eggs I put up with this cure, but soon gave that up as the small eggs simply lacked enough skein to keep them together.

Silver salmon eggs have proven the most productive because they are at the ideal stage of development, meaning the egg-to-skein ratio is optimal, and they have terrific color. We'd pick up silver eggs while fishing the coast; if we didn't catch enough hens we would await incoming boats, offering to clean their fish in return for the eggs. Also, if heading to Alaska in midsummer, bringing back a five-gallon bucket full of rich-colored silver eggs can lead to good fishing on local streams.

Winter steelhead eggs are the next choice. Sexually, the fish have matured and the eggs are of perfect size. Ensconced in the thick, membranous skein they stay on through numerous casts.

Spring chinook eggs are a close third. If taken a bit later in the season they are great, for the growing cells are still firmly set in a sturdy skein. Though a bit small, summer steelhead eggs are also effective. They are extremely tough, withstanding many casts.

Fall chinook are nearing the spawning period and their skeins are quite large. This means less of an egg-to-skein ratio. These make wonderful baits if you're pulling Mudbugs or backbouncing through deep salmon holes, but don't work worth a darn in rushing riffles.

When curing fall chinook eggs, we often cure the whole skein in one piece or cut it in half. This allows the eggs contacting the skein to setup rather than being jostled loose by excessive handling when the skein is wet. Once hardened, the inner, loose eggs are worked free and the baits cut to desired size.

Concluding thoughts

Now that you're ready to hit the river, there's a basic, yet often overlooked rule when it comes to getting the most out of your bait. When putting your egg cluster in the egg-loop, be sure the skein is against the egg-loop and eye of the hook. This will cinch the eggs snugly into the skein and avoid them being severed by the line.

Don't be afraid to experiment with small quantities of eggs. For salmon fishing, I like large baits cured fairly wet as they milk out well in deep, swirling holes. If I'm fishing fast water, I prefer the eggs a bit more firm, to resist punishment. For steelhead, I like small, hard baits not only because they hold up in rushing water, but because they stay on longer when trout pester them. You may find a combination that works better for you, given the fish you are after and the water in which you pursue them.

Don't hesitate to give this cure a try. I've tested several recipes over the years but always go back to the one I first put to use 30 years ago; it still catches fish.

The author has taken more salmon and steelhead on this cure than all others he's used, combined.

Kenai River Magnum Baits for Magnum Fish

INGREDIENTS

- 1/2 cup Pro-Cure
- Kenai Cocktail Juice
- Slam-Ola Powder
- Oils of choice
  (sardine, shrimp, DMSO, garlic, etc.)

The first time I fished with Alaskan guide, Brett Gesh on the world-famous Kenai River, I thought he was nuts using egg clusters the size of baseballs. He'd alerted me to the fact we'd be using big baits, but when he handed me the first one, it caught me off guard. A single bait cradled in the egg loop of a 7/0 Gamakatsu hook barely fits into the palm of a grown man's hand.

The Kenai is a fastflowing river, and wimpy baits get shredded in minutes. If the bait does not stay fresh and intact, your chances of hooking that potential world-record dramatically decreases. Each bait is carefully cut to ensure optimum skein is attached, so as to remain on the hook as long as possible.

One of these giant clusters would yield up to a dozen of my regular size, spring chinook baits. Gesh started using magnum baits in 1995, during the month bait-fishing became legal on the river. Immediately he had success. There are few secrets on the Kenai and soon other guides were using larger baits and having increased success, though some still struggle with the idea of using bait to match the size of what Gesh uses.

If you're apprehensive about large baits, pry open the mouth of the next big king you come across. "I first tried big baits when I sat down and really studied how big a 50-pound king's mouth is. Getting a 9/0 hook into a fish that large would be no problem," comments Gesh. "I believe, the bigger the bait, the more scent you introduce into the water. This is critical for increasing the visibility of eggs and the amount of scent you introduce into the river."

I've known Gesh most of my life, but my last fishing trip with him on the Kenai was what every salmon fanatic dreams about. In three days of fishing, we hooked 20 kings and landed 15, all between 40 and 70 pounds. Granted, this was an exceptional few days of fishing, but Gesh had consistent success throughout the 2001 season. His clients landed 141 kings, seven of which were over 70 pounds while about 40% of the fish tagged eclipsed the 50-pound mark. He credits much of this success to his magnum baits and cures.

Remember, in fishing the lower Kenai, these salmon are fresh from salt. They can be ravenous feeders with voracious appetites. A big, quality bait not only attracts their attention, it seems to entice them into biting.

Like many anglers these days, Gesh begins with Pro-Cure for the simple reason it's quick, easy, and effective. Gesh begins by cutting his baits into fishable sizes – about the size of a tennis ball or baseball – and fills a one-gallon Ziploc bag 1/4 of the way up with the baits. He then sprinkles 1/2 cup or so of Pro-Cure into the bag, thoroughly mixing it up. If you want more cure to soak in, simply add more.

Taking a bottle of Pro-Cure's Kenai Cocktail Juice, Gesh mixes 3-4 ounces into the bag. Then he adds a generous portion of Pro-Cure's Slam-Ola powder. You can add as much as you'd like, but a half-cup should do the trick.

Gesh prefers his eggs to be extremely wet for salmon fishing, with no crust whatsoever on the outside (he makes them firmer for steelhead by allowing time to air dry), so he leaves them in the bags in which they were cured. When fishing, he'll place the bags in a cooler, working directly from the pink, saturated bags. It should be mentioned, this is a messy process. Gesh is already getting ribbed by fellow guides for his pink boat, stained that hue

Brett Gesh puts up hundreds of pounds of Kenai king eggs each summer. These eggs are from one day's catch.

due to the amount of Pro-Cure he liberally applies. When I fished with him, Gesh was covered from head to toe in pink stain; his boat gunnels, deck, and rods also glowed of the pink stuff. Needless to say, he wears his rain gear, even on sunny days. Eventually the pink does wash off the boat, thanks to the customized washdown pump Gesh had installed in his RB Boat.

Though Gesh keeps no secrets when it comes to his cures, if he had one element to share that could benefit all of us, it would be his use of oils. Gesh is a radical oil and scent man. From Smelly Jelly (the only non Pro-Cure product he uses) to the vast array of oils created by Pro-Cure, Gesh is always experimenting with his cures. He loves sardine, shrimp, garlic and DMSO oils, to name a few.

A deadly combination: Pro-Cure scents and Slam-Ola powder. Gesh believes Slam-Ola to be one of the best kept 'secrets' in the world of fishing.

"I like trying to match my oils with what fish are feeding on," offers Gesh. "If you're going to be fishing regularly, try three cures, each with different oil mixtures. By using at least three different oils, you have a better chance of finding what fish desire. Don't be afraid to experiment. Once you get a rod that's producing, stick with it that day, for the next time that one might not be the hot stick."

Gesh carries a powerful belief when it comes to breaking new ground. He's always experimenting with novel ideas in his cures, be it oils, curing time or how long he keeps a bait in the water. The days I last fished with him, baits were brought in every 15 minutes to be recharged. Gesh puts the egg cluster back in the curing bag from which it came, and puts on a new bait to fish with. This freshens the baits, allowing cure, scent, and oils to penetrate the egg's membrane.

By constantly freshening his baits, Gesh believes he increases their fishing range. Oils in cures are for dispersing scent from the eggs. Without the oils, Gesh feels he may be only fishing a one-foot swath of water as the bait travels downstream. With the oils, he broadens his fishing range to a three-foot swath — a definite advantage in Alaska's glaciated waters where visibility is minimal. Constantly recharging baits takes time and effort, and results in a pinker boat than some may desire, but it catches fish.

"You've gotta believe in what you're fishing with," advises Gesh.

"I judge my success by the eggs I use, not the style of fishing I do. Divers, backbouncing, Kwikfish, and so forth are all productive methods, but if I don't have fresh, well-cured eggs on the end of my line, my confidence level drops considerably. That's one reason why I'm constantly changing things around, I never want to settle for one set way of doing things on the river. You never know, there could be something better that no one's tried yet."

Guides like Gesh, who work big rivers every day of the season, often go without having to freeze any eggs. If you must freeze your eggs using the recipe Gesh provided, it's best done without the oils. Oils don't freeze, so place the eggs in the freezer with only the Pro-Cure in the bag. When you're ready to fish, remove the eggs, let them create their own juices, then add oils.

Big baits treated in Pro-Cure are to what Gesh credits much of his angling success.

You can also vacuum seal this cure, but you must freeze them first. The eggs are so plump and soft, putting them under pressure in a vacuum sealer causes hemorrhaging. It's advisable to freeze the eggs in a plastic bag, then take them out of the bag and vacuum seal them. When ready to fish, thaw the eggs out, pour the contents into a large, workable baggy, add more Pro-Cure to dry up the baits a bit as they'll be quite soggy, then add oils as needed.

Gesh has also used this cure on Oregon's Elk River with great success. Though he downsized the bait to fit on a 5/0 hook, they were still large by Elk standards. The cure on these magnum baits produced when nothing else would.

Not only does Gesh specialize in giant king salmon, he nails monster rainbows and Dolly Varden on the Kenai, and gets his fair share of silver, red, and pink salmon. This guy works as hard as anyone I've fished with, and his results speak for themselves.

Alaskan guide, Brett Gesh, with a prized Kenai king. Gesh believes his egg cure is one of the major factors leading him to so many big fish.

3:2:1...Buzz!

INGREDIENTS
- 3 parts borax
- 2 parts sugar
- 1 part noniodized salt
- Optional dyes and scents

When it comes to salmon and steelhead fishing, Buzz Ramsey is an icon. Although not a guide, Buzz has spent a lot of time on the rivers fishing and promoting the products made by Luhr-Jensen. Currently, he manages sales and promotions for Luhr-Jensen & Sons, Incorporated. Since 1974 Buzz has been affiliated with the fishing business megagiant and during that time managed to earn himself a household name through sport fishing.

Born in Toledo, Oregon in 1950, Buzz was part of an outdoor family from the start. Today, his biographical sketch reads like a "Who' s-Who" among anglers. Not only does Buzz present seminars, produce instructional videos, and write regular outdoor columns for newspapers in the Pacific Northwest, but he's designed lures and introduced new styles of fishing to people across the nation. In 1995, Buzz was inducted into the National Fresh Water Fishing Hall of Fame, and in 1996, the Northwest Steelheaders Hall of Fame.

I feel fortunate in having Buzz impart his wisdom on egg cures for this book–something he was more than willing to do. "If it will help people catch fish, count me in," commented Buzz when I asked if he'd be willing to share a recipe.

The ingredients for this recipe are easy to attain.

"I'll tell ya right off, I have no secret, magical cures," began Ramsey. "I use the same gear as most people, right down to my eggs. One of my favorite cures is basic, but I do a few things different than some folks which may be why they've been so productive for me over the years."

In a large, bucket-sized container, Buzz mixes three parts borax, two parts sugar, and one part salt. He likes having a lot of this cure on hand, ready to go, so he doesn't have to mix the ingredients every time he needs to put up eggs.

As you'll read throughout this book, Ramsey agrees that working with clean, blood-free eggs is the first step in obtaining a quality bait. To make your skeins easy to handle, cut each into either three or six manageable pieces. The number of pieces you have will be dictated by the size of the skeins. Large skeins, like those from chinook, can be cut lengthwise first, then divided into three equal sections. When making this cut, be sure to slice the skeins from the open side so that each lengthwise piece will have enough connecting membrane to hold them together. Average size skeins, like those from normal size coho or steelhead, need not be split and should be cut into three equal sections. With proper cuts made, place the manageable pieces on butcher paper.

Buzz Ramsey believes in clipping the blood-tainted ends of his skeins before curing.

Sprinkle the eggs with a light coating of cure, rolling them in the powder to make certain all surfaces are covered. This is how mom used to flour chicken. Make sure and get some cure down into each egg layer, then dump all of the baits into a Tupperware container and place in the refrigerator. During this stage, juices will begin to form. If lots of juice is created, gently mix the eggs to encourage reabsorption of the liquid.

"If you're looking for a more durable egg or if you want to reduce the size of overly ripe eggs, you can pour off some of the liquid, which will help toughen them up," offers Ramsey. "After 24 hours of sitting in the refrigerator, when the majority of juices have bled from the eggs, you can add liquid dyes as well as scents. Shrimp, herring, and anise oil are just a few of the choices out there. As for dyes, reds and oranges are popular, but the degree of richness is up to the individual curing the eggs." Introduce dyes and scents once the eggs have created their own juices because at this stage the cells begin reabsorbing lost fluids. The ultimate goal is to have scent and color drawn back into the cells during the plasmolysis phase, thus producing an egg that holds its color, milks well, and distributes scent in the process.

"I'll keep these eggs curing in the refrigerator for three days," claims Ramsey. "When the time is up, I'll stick the entire container in the freezer. This cure has such a high sugar and salt content that the eggs rarely freezer burn. In fact, I once mistakenly left the lid off an egg container and didn't discover it for months as it was shoved to the back of the freezer. Despite being covered with an inch of frost buildup, they showed no signs of burning. Though this is not the ideal scenario to have happen, it shows how, if mixed accurately, this cure can't go wrong."

Buzz has learned it's best to utilize the eggs from this cure within a year of being processed. He's also observed that when stored in the freezer, chinook eggs appear to outlast other salmon and steelhead eggs treated in this recipe. Buzz is particularly fond of this cure as all eggs from all salmon and steelhead react well to the ratios of ingredients. Ramsey says the eggs put up in this cure can be fished by any method, be it plunking, sidecasting, backbouncing, or working them behind divers.

When preparing to fish these baits, Buzz typically cuts the clusters into desired sizes once he's on the river. "When handling baits on the river, don't be afraid to get a bit of cure on your boat," suggests Ramsey. "One thing I see more and more boat anglers doing lately is placing their cluster in their egg loop, then dropping it over the edge while they clean their hands. Don't do it! Baits are most effective in their first few casts. When you give them time to milk out while washing your hands, you're decreasing their overall potency before even getting started," notes Ramsey.

Once you're baited up, let the terminal tackle dangle in the air or sit on a towel while you clean your hands. Attention to such detail takes

An angler putting his fresh bait in water while washing his hands is something Ramsey sees too much of, and which he cautions anglers to avoid.

minimal effort, and could mean the difference between catching and not catching fish.

On a final note, Ramsey reflected, "There's a lot to be said about different cures. Not all fish will eat the same thing every day, which is why I take multiple cures with me when I go fishing. Like many guys, I have some baits mixed with different oils and scents that I'll try when other cures aren't working. Don't limit yourself to any one cure; find a few you like and stick with those. The more diverse your approach, the greater your chances of hooking fish."

Boiled Eggs

INGREDIENTS

- 1 cup sugar
- Borax
- 1 quart water
- 1 cup noniodized salt
- 1 packet of cherry flavored Kool-Aid
- 1 large skein of eggs

The following recipe is a favorite of seasoned angler Mike Schoby. Mike was born and raised in Washington, where he's chased salmon and steelhead since he was a boy. Some of Mike's fondest memories are of pursuing steelhead in many of Washington's famous rivers. Hitting bruiser winter steelhead and furious-fighting summer runs on the Cowlitz make up some of his most cherished recollections. The cures described in the next two chapters, topped with a single Corky, continue to work wonders for Schoby.

Before becoming a Cabela's employee, Schoby spent a great deal of time guiding big-game hunts and fishing trips in Africa. He frequently visits home, and when he does, it's tough reaching him because he's likely on the river.

Schoby prefers to rinse his eggs, removing any blood.

Be it fishing in his home state, or anywhere else in the world where Mike finds salmon and steelhead, he likes rolling eggs. Over the years, Mike has taken some impressive fish on these cures, both in size and number.

Begin by thoroughly washing the skeins to remove any traces of blood, then pat the eggs dry with a paper towel. Using kitchen shears, cut the eggs into desired bait size. The size of baits are determined by the condition of the eggs you are curing, what species you intend on fishing for and in what types of water you'll be fishing.

Next, mix all of the ingredients (except for the borax and egg chunks) and bring to a boil. Allow the mixture to boil until all items are dissolved. After everything is dissolved, allow the brine to cool to a warm temperature. When you can comfortably place your

Boiling key ingredients is what Mike Schoby has found to be most effective with this cure.

hand in the brine, carefully add the eggs. Let the eggs soak for 30-45 minutes.

Remove the egg clusters from the brine and place them on a mesh tray to dry. This can be done outside, or over a sink if your wife is understanding. Let the eggs drip dry for a couple of hours, or until they feel tacky to the touch.

Gently pick up the egg clusters and place on paper towels. Put them in the refrigerator for 10 to 15 hours. The cold, dry environment will expedite in setting up and drying the eggs. If you want them moist, remove them sooner. If you desire hard eggs, say for fishing fast water, you may want to leave them in longer.

Removing the baits from the refrigerator, roll each one in borax, then place it in Tupperware container or vacuum-sealed pouch. Immediately place in the freezer or take fishing, as they are ready to use.

Once cured, these eggs can be frozen up to two years and will still milk well once they hit the river. Mike has learned that freezing the eggs in small packages is ideal, for once they are thawed they should not be refrozen. Even when they are kept cool they have a relatively short life, so you'll want to use up your thawed baits in a day or two.

A Dry Kool-Aid Mix

INGREDIENTS

- 1 cup borax
- 1/2 cup salt
- 1 cup sugar
- 1 packet Kool-Aid
- Shrimp oil

Mike Schoby also has a simple recipe that's proven very successful over the years. It's fairly fast, easy, and works well when there's simply not enough time to devote to his recipe in the previous chapter.

Begin by mixing the sugar, borax, salt and Kool-Aid in a bowl. Cut your eggs into desired bait sizes. Place the eggs, along with the cure, into a plastic bag. Gently but thoroughly shake the plastic bag to ensure all parts of the eggs are completely covered in the mixture.

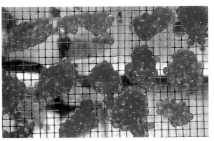

Placing eggs to dry so air can circulate around all parts, is an important step in this cure.

Once covered with the cure, remove the eggs and place them on a mesh tray or screen, with a catch basin or newspapers below to collect any drainage. Place the tray in the refrigerator for 10-15 hours.

Sprinkle a layer of borax in the bottom of a small Tupperware or plastic container and cover with eggs. Apply one or two drops of shrimp oil over this layer. Repeat the layering and oil process until the container is full or you're out of eggs, then finish it off with a layer of borax. Place the container in the freezer until you're ready to go. This cure holds up well and milks out good.

A very natural egg cluster is the end result of this cure. Mike Schoby especially likes this recipe on steelhead.

A Versatile Cure

INGREDIENTS
- 2 cups borax
- 1/2 cup noniodized salt
- 1 cup sugar
- 1/2 cup Pro-Cure dye
- Optional oils

If you've been searching for a versatile cure, one that allows you to experiment with colors, toughness, oils and scents, this is it. It's quick, easy, and presents many options to the curious angler intent on trying several new variations within a base-cure.

This cure comes from veteran guide Mike Bogue, of Redding, California. Bogue spends most of his time guiding on the world-renowned Sacramento River. He's used this cure extensively on salmon and steelhead. This is one of his favorite cures to use on mature chinook eggs, but it works well on all other eggs as well. The only change Bogue makes when curing steelhead eggs is omitting the dye, feeling the egg's natural color is hard to beat.

Bogue is a believer in having three or four cures to fish each time he sets foot on the river. "One day the bite may be hot on shrimp oil, the next day those eggs may not raise a fish. If they go cold, I'll try another scent on my eggs," Bogue says.

It's that sort of diversity that makes Bogue an effective guide, and this cure so special.

Mike Bogue's willingness to experiment with a wide variety of scents is critical to his success.

Start by taking two cups of borax, a half cup of salt, one cup of sugar, and a half cup Pro-Cure Dye and mix them into a gallon-sized Ziploc bag. Shake the contents well. Next, cut the skeins into fourths, or manageable sized pieces. Place each quarter skein in the bag, one at a time, gently rolling it around until it's totally covered in powder. Remove that quarter-skein and repeat with the remaining quarter sections of skein. There is enough ingredients in this one-gallon bag to cure up to four large mature salmon skeins.

Once removed from the bag, place the eggs on a drying screen. Bogue uses a 2' x3'screen with 1/4" holes. Bogue's screen has a wooden frame to allow him to move it around with ease. You may choose a different-sized screen, but make sure the holes are large enough to allow air to move under and around the eggs.

The eggs typically remain on the rack overnight. Test them to the touch. If they are too soft, let them dry a bit longer. Usually, 10-15 hours of drying at room temperature is all it takes.

"When they've reached the desired texture, I like wrapping the eggs in paper towels and putting them in Tupperware containers in the refrigerator," claims Bogue. "When they've dried, they are ready to fish, and I've used them that fast with very good success. But if I have a few extra days in which I'm not desperate for eggs, I prefer letting them stay in the 'fridge a few days, to more fully set up."

When Bogue takes to the river, he'll cut these 1/4 size skeins into fishable baits. His bait size depends on the fish he's after and the type of water he's fishing, thus the delay in cutting his eggs.

Working at room temperature is preferred. In fact, during those hot summer evenings Redding is famous for, Bogue won't put his eggs to cure until nightfall, after temperatures have dropped considerably. Likewise, if you live in a humid region, it will take quite a bit longer for this cure to set up. Bogue notes that in the fall and winter months, when the air is heavy with moisture, it takes the eggs longer to achieve the right texture. In fact, it can take an extra three days to achieve the perfect stage.

Once the eggs set up, the beauty of this cure comes in. Within each individual carton, Bogue likes experimenting with various oils. One container may be targeted for shrimp oil, others will have crawdad, sardine, anchovy oil, or DMSO. Other oils and scents – either on their own or in combination – can also be experimented with. It may be, you want to add anise oil or garlic scent to your shrimp-oiled eggs. You can see how quickly the variations on this simple recipe can multiply.

Bogue advises those tinkering with several different cures to take the time and clearly label them. If you're putting up lots of eggs, it's easy to forget what you have in the back of the refrigerator. You may have a half-dozen modifications of this cure simultaneously processing and you don't want to mix them up or forget where you are at this critical stage.

As for Bogue's preferred type of Pro-Cure Bait Dye, he likes Radiant Red Fluorescent. Red is a tough color to beat on the Sacramento and this is Bogue's money color. He's also had good success with the Fire Orange Fluorescent.

For an added twist when mixing his dry brine in the Ziploc bag, Bogue will often add a generous portion of Slam-Ola. He has noted instant results switching to eggs cured in this brine when nothing else on the river produced.

As for salt portions, Bogue has learned that the more mature and

Adding scents to the finished cure is an important step many anglers believe in; Bogue agrees.

loose the eggs, the more salt you'll want to add. This makes the eggs nice and tight, so they stay fishable for a longer period of time. At the same time, if the eggs you're curing are young and firm, you may want to go lighter on the salt as the extra shrinking will not be necessary.

Bogue was born and raised in Redding, California and has fished his entire life. He's been guiding here since 1990, primarily concentrating on the salmon, trout, and steelhead of the Sacramento River, 150-200 miles from the ocean. The volume of fish on this river doesn't necessitate his looking elsewhere to wet a line. The 2001 season was one of the best on the river, with 50-and 60-pound kings routinely being coughed up. In spring, Bogue concentrates on big beautiful rainbows, while the fall and winter months find him chasing steelhead as well as salmon. It's a unique fishery, indeed.

Photo Mike Bogue

One of Mike Bogue's happy clients with a Sacramento River chinook.

Half-N-Half and Careful Handling

INGREDIENTS
- Quick Cure
- Pro Glow
- Optional oils

A true ambassador to sport fishing, guide Chris Vertopoulos, of Northwest Angling Experience, epitomizes what life is about. Unlike many in his profession, Chris has little to hide. He was a self-taught angler and honed his skills to a level of proficiency that now allows him to make a living at it. He's learned a lot about fishing from experts and other people in the industry, and to them he is ever grateful. He's also adamant about passing on to others what he has learned, so they too may obtain fulfillment on the water.

Nobody in his family fished, and as a kid, Chris acquired a great deal of knowledge through reading and research. He still has his collection of STS Magazines, dating back to the mid-1970s and claims this magazine has helped him more than any other.

When I asked Chris to share his favorite egg-curing secrets, he replied, "I have nothing to hide. Though I do have one recipe I can't share as I was sworn to secrecy from the man who gave it to me, I don't necessarily consider it my best cure." In fact, Chris' favorite cure is simple, the result of many seasons of experimenting around on his own.

Chris believes most prepackaged, all-in-one cures now on the market are good ones, as their sulfite bases make them ideal for enticing salmon and steelhead. The only difference he sees is that some have stronger attributes in certain areas than others. He also feels the handling process, before and after the eggs have cured, is critical to producing quality baits.

His preferred cure is simple: 1/2 Quick Cure, 1/2 Pro Glow Egg Cure. "Quick Cure alone does not have the coloring I desire, while Pro Glow alone has too much sugar to my liking," comments Chris. "But mix them half-and-half and you have a deadly cure."

Like most anglers, Chris believes the handling process is crucial in obtaining a quality egg. Any hen he catches, be it salmon or steelhead, he immediately conks on the head and slits both gills. Within 24 hours his eggs are curing. He doesn't refrigerate, freeze, or even rinse the eggs off with water.

After bleeding the fish, he'll remove the eggs and wrap each skein in a

While on the river, Chris Vertopoulos prefers removing the eggs with gloved hands, blotting them with a paper towel and placing them in sealable baggies.

paper towel to absorb the blood and bacteria, then place them in Ziploc bags. Lots of bacteria can move from the gut onto the eggs, and once bacteria penetrates the eggs, they will become tainted. Because water and eggs don't mix, Chris is against rinsing them, feeling paper towels are better for lifting the blood and bacteria from the raw skein. He also feels dipping skeins in water before they cure softens the eggs, as the possibility of water seeping into the cells can make them weaker to work with. With his skeins now in the bags to dry, Chris gets back to fishing.

When fishing, Chris washes his hands several times a day to reduce the likelihood of human odors interfering with his baits. Lemon Joy is a favorite of his, as it is with many guides, though any unscented soap should suffice. This cleanliness carries over to removing and handling eggs that are drawn from any fish he catches.

Chris will not work with frozen skeins of uncured eggs. His reasoning makes sense, for as water in the cells freeze, the membranes expand, causing microscopic fractures to form. This causes the eggs to become extremely fragile; many even burst, rendering them useless.

Once home and ready to cure his eggs, Chris grabs the skeins and clips both ends of the long, often blood-filled vein running lengthwise through the skein. He then forces the blood from this vein and cuts the skeins into golfball-sized clusters. If fishing for steelhead, simply cut the baits smaller when the time comes.

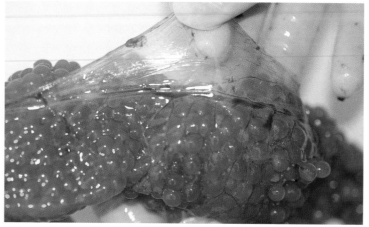

Clipping the vein running through the skein is important to Vertopoulos. This promotes a blood-free egg prior to curing.

With the baits placed in a tub, Chris sprinkles the cure over them and thoroughly mixes it into every fold by hand. Wearing gloves is critical when touching the cure. If you desire chemically hotter, brighter eggs, simply add a bit more cure, but be careful not to add too much, for fear of burning the eggs. Now place the eggs in a jar, where they will be rotated every hour or so to keep the juices reabsorbing into the cells. This is done for a few hours, or until you go to bed.

In the morning, gently dump the eggs into a colander and strain the excess liquid. Place the eggs on the 1/4" screen with a drip pan or newspapers beneath them. Chris sets a fan to low speed, allowing it to blow directly on the eggs for one hour. At the end of an hour, flip the eggs over and keep the fan on for another hour. If they are to your desired texture, the eggs can now be frozen. Caution must be taken not to overdo it on the fan, you don't want to dry the eggs out.

If he'll use the eggs within a week, Chris stores them in the refrigerator. For long-term storage, the eggs need to be kept in the freezer. He prefers vacuum sealing them in jars, where he has kept them safely in the freezer for up to three years.

When fishing this cure, Chris will often change his eggs, to ensure a fresh bait is out there. The fresher the bait, the more actively it will milk, the better the chances of attracting fish.

Chris even uses this cure for steelhead. "While many people will not fish sulfite cures for steelhead, I've had good luck with this one on both summer and winter steelhead," Chris attests. "I just make it a point to go light on the cure when putting up eggs I know I'll use for steelhead. I apply just enough to get color into the eggs. Though lots of guys prefer borax cures for steelies – claiming they produce a harder egg, thus holding up better in fast water – I've had good success with this one."

Vertopoulos' recipe yields very rich colored eggs.

He's also very pleased with the way this cure works on all eggs: silvers, chinook, reds, pinks, chum, and steelhead. Chris does not hesitate in utilizing all of these species of fish eggs on both salmon and steelhead.

An easy twist to this cure when in the juicing stage, is adding a few drops of shrimp oil to the mix. "Go light on the oils," Chris warns. "You don't want an oil slick coming off your bait, when that happens, all the scent from the egg is being carried atop the water," Chris offers. "The milking ability of an egg is vital to a fish's visual and olfactory senses. If these scents float up with the oil, the fish can't detect them as well."

Vertopoulos was born and raised in Vancouver, Washington. He's been fishing southwest Washington and northwest Oregon rivers for over two decades. His guiding responsibilities have taken him to various places in Alaska as well. Chris now focuses most of his attention on Oregon streams, where he pursues spring chinook before turning to sturgeon in the summer. He then hits chinook and coho in late summer and through the fall, before concentrating on winter steelhead well into March.

Leon Zalcow, one of Chris Vertopoulos' clients, with a Sandy River spring chinook taken on the egg cure described in this chapter.

Photo, Chris Vertopoulos

Keep the Shaker Full

INGREDIENTS
- 1 cup sodium sulfite
- 1/2 cup sugar
- 1/2 cup noniodized salt

One of the hardest-working – and most successful – fishermen I know is Steve Rich. Throughout the 1980s and into the '90s, Rich guided salmon, steelhead, and trout anglers throughout the state of Oregon. He's noted for a fishing hole on Oregon's famed Smith River that now bears his name. In one day, Rich and his two clients landed 60 winter steelhead – in one hole!

Many of the fish taken that day, and throughout his guiding career, fell to a simple cure Rich still uses. Though he's no longer an active guide, Rich is on the river every chance he gets.

This cure has a high concentration of sodium sulfite, but Rich likes it because it turns the eggs a brilliant color, they milk very well, and the baits are tough which is ideal for sidecasting. He's used it extensively on spring and fall chinook as well as summer and winter steelhead.

Mix one cup sodium sulfite, a half cup sugar, and a half cup salt into an oversized salt shaker. As in all cures, the sulfite acts as a color preservative, the sugar a hardener, and the salt to draw liquid

The recipe of Steve Rich utilizes a full cup of sodium sulfite, an extreme he adheres to no matter what kind of eggs he's curing.

from the cells and preserve the eggs. Having a large, sealed container of this cure on hand during the time lots of fish are being caught can be a time saver so you don't have to spend time mixing the ingredients. Simply refill the shaker and you're set.

Take the skeins of eggs and cut them into desired bait sizes. Rich likes cutting the eggs before they are cured as they are more stable and less likely to rupture. Place the baits on a broiling pan or mesh screen with a catch basin beneath. Lay out the individual baits atop the rack and sprinkle with the cure.

Apply enough cure to coat the eggs with a light covering of white. Let the eggs sit overnight, or about 12 hours. The following day, flip each bait, cover with cure again, and either let them sit or fish them.

After the second application of the cure, the eggs are ready to fish. They can be placed in small baggies and taken to the river, or placed in the freezer. If a firmer egg is what you're after, let them air dry until they reach the desired texture, then bag and freeze. Once on the river, oils and scents can be added.

Rich has kept eggs from this cure in the freezer for up to two years, and they fished with good results. If you have the ingredients mixed early on, this is a simple cure that requires little attention and produces fish.

A natural-looking bait that milks out well is the product of this cure.

T-N-T...It's Dynamite

INGREDIENTS
- T-N-T Cure

Prepackaged cures are a popular trend on the market; some are more than a trend, they are here to stay. These cures are becoming famous because they are quick and easy to work with. All of the ingredients come in one package, all you have to do is add eggs. These cures are real time savers, and if used properly, are very effective.

T-N-T Egg Cure is one of the most recent prepackaged cures to hit the market, and it's proving to be deadly. Designed by Todd Allen, an ardent angler living in Sweet Home, Oregon, T-N-T will likely be around for many years. Allen has experimented with egg cures since moving to Oregon in 1979, but five years ago became set on developing the ultimate cure. For five years he worked with the cure he now markets. It took two years to get the cure where he wanted it, then three more years of extensive testing to see how it performed. Satisfied with his results, Allen made his T-N-T cure available to the public for the first time in the summer of 2001.

Allen did all the leg work and research for this product himself, and what he came away with is impressive. He began by evaluating all the cures he could get his hands on. He even went so far as to carry out taste tests to decipher what ingredients were in other cures, despite what label warnings said.

T-N-T is a sulfite-based cure with its share of nitrates. "I like sulfite cures for salmon because it's not only a preservative, but it's also found in commercial fish foods," states Allen. "I'm a firm believer that returning salmon sense the sulfite smell in these baits because it's what they were raised on in hatcheries. The sulfite base may not produce every time out, but that's where it's nice to have the nitrates for insurance."

In the spring of 2001, Allen boated 149 salmon on T-N-T from Oregon's South Santiam River, including 22 in one day. Though he's not a guide, Allen is starting to cure eggs for a selection of professionals. Early in the 2002 season, one guide using T-N-T hooked 32 winter steelhead in three days. Another guide was struggling on spring chinook, and after an extensive dry spell sought Allen's cure. The next day the guide nailed five springers. The rest is history.

Though these figures are impressive, it wasn't the numbers of fish taken that initially caught my attention, rather how the eggs from this cure displayed amazing stamina under extreme conditions. Dave Jones, manager of Midway Sports Center in Sweet Home, was putting up 45 pounds of eggs with T-N-T. Within an hour of sprinkling the cure into a five gallon bucket of eggs, 10-12 inches of juice came to the top. Jones occasionally mixed the cure over the next three days, at which time all of the juices reabsorbed into the eggs.

Jones then rinsed the eggs, losing a few berries in the gravel. For seven days these forgotten eggs laid in the rocks, getting baked by the sun. Then it rained. Walking in his driveway, Jones didn't think anything about the eggs until he observed a stream of white in a tiny puddle of water. Closer inspection revealed plump, vibrant eggs, slowly releasing their contents. Through observation, Jones discovered that the eggs continued to milk for three more days. This shows how T-N-T penetrates and remains in the cells, even after being dried out.

Intent on learning more about this cure and the handling process, I spoke with Allen. He explained the process he likes applying when using T-N-T Egg Cure. Begin by butterflying the skein, that is, cutting it down the middle of the unskeined side and opening it up. Sprinkle T-N-T into the open eggs and rub into every crevice. Be sure to wear gloves, Allen warns, as this stuff stains terribly. Place the covered skeins into a gallon Ziploc bag and let sit at room temperature. Every 15-30 minutes, gently massage the bags to stimulate juicing. In about three hours, when the juices flow and the nitrates and sulfites start penetrating the eggs, flip the bag around, completely mixing the eggs and the cure.

Massaging T-N-T into every fold is what Todd Allen believes necessary to achieve a fully cured skein.

Let them sit 12-15 hours, then remove the eggs and let air dry on white, unscented paper towels. The use of newspaper is ill-advised as sulfites and chemicals in the cure will pull the ink off the paper, thus tainting the eggs. Let the eggs dry until sticky to the touch, then fish or freeze them.

If making steelhead baits, Allen prefers cutting them to about thumbnail size. He then rolls the little clusters in borax powder to toughen them up. Allowing the baits time to firm up will ensure a tougher egg that will better withstand steelhead waters.

When vacuum sealed and stored in the freezer, these eggs will last for years. Eggs from this cure hold together extremely well for drift fishing and backbouncing. Allen catches 99% of his salmon by fishing these eggs with a bobber. He'll leave the same bait on for up to 30 minutes.

If you want to add oils or scents, it's best done two or three hours into the process, when juices are being created. This way, when osmosis occurs within the cells, scent along with protoplasm will undergo plasmolysis, locking them inside the cell walls. When working with oils, though, Allen believes too much will make the eggs soft, so use sparingly.

T-N-T is currently available in three colors: Radiant Orange, Radical Red, and Natural Glow. For salmon, Allen prefers using Radical Red to turn his eggs a purple color. He likes the more subtle hue, for in clear water he's actually witnessed salmon spooking when the Radical Red was presented to them. For steelhead, he's had extensive success on all three types.

T-N-T is also great for curing prawns. Using a heavy application, let the prawns sit in the cure for 24 hours. This will ensure ample time for the crustaceans to become impregnated with all scents and firm up. It's also very good for toughening up herring.

T-N-T is available through Midway Sports Center. Refer to the appendix for contact details. Available in 15 ounce bottles, this is enough to cure between 35 and 45 pounds of eggs.

T-N-T produces attractive baits that many salmon and steelhead anglers throughout the West are having good luck on.

A Dry Cure Good to Go

INGREDIENTS

- 1 1/2 cups borax
- 1/2 cup sugar
- 1 tablespoon sodium sulfite
- 1 tablespoon of Wizard Cure
  (Hot Lava by Pro-Cure)

Rinsing eggs of any unwanted residue, prior to curing, is a step Gary Thomas takes.

A fishing fiend when it comes to salmon and steelhead, Gary Thomas of Springfield, Oregon, travels the Pacific Northwest in search of fish. A science teacher by profession, he could be a top-notch guide if he so desired. My dad and I have fished with Gary for over twenty years, and this guy knows his stuff.

Thomas is one who is constantly experimenting with his egg cures. Last I spoke with him, he was trying grounded, processed fish foods in his cure, to see if hatchery – stock fish carried with them any recollections of the foods they ate as fingerlings. It's this type of experimentation to which Thomas credits much of his fishing success, and he rates a good cured egg among the most vital fishing tool a person can have.

Thomas shared two of his favorite cures. In his dry cure, Thomas thoroughly mixes the ingredients listed above. He then cuts them into fishable-size baits or splits the skeins lengthwise, right up the middle. In larger, fall chinook skeins, he'll get four strips of eggs per skein from these mature fish. Next, place the skeins in a plastic tub, loose eggs facing up.

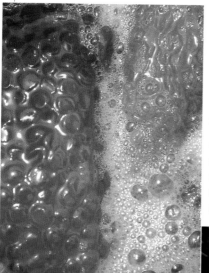

Once juicing begins, Thomas advocates occasionally stirring the eggs.

Heavily sprinkle the mixed cure over the eggs until they are evenly covered. Let set for 12 hours at room temperature. Once the eggs start producing juice, periodically "pan" or baste the fluids over the eggs to carry color into the cells. After 12 hours, remove the eggs and rinse with ice-cold water. Rinsing with cold water sets the eggs and rids them of the sugar crust that forms.

Thomas uses Wizard Cure to add color to eggs put up in this cure.

Once clean, drain and pat the cured eggs dry and place on white paper towels to air dry. Keeping the eggs at room temperature during this stage seems to work best. Allow the eggs to sit for as long as you desire. The longer they sit, the harder they become. If you're fishing fast, heavy water, you'll want a drier bait that stays on longer. If you're fishing with bobbers, a large, soft bait is what you want.

When removed from the solution, Thomas rinses the eggs under ice-cold water. This sets the eggs and rids them of any crystallization.

After the eggs have reached the desired dryness, place them in jars and refrigerate overnight to give all the eggs the same consistency. The next morning they are ready to fish or freeze. If cured in skeins or strips of skeins, you can cut them to bait size either before freezing them or when you're on the river. Thomas vacuum seals his eggs in pint or quart-sized jars. Vacuum sealing the baits in jars retards freezer burn and considerably prolongs the life of the eggs.

If the frozen eggs in the sealed jars start turning white, simply thaw and turn over to let the juices filter through. You want to get the juices reabsorbed into the eggs to lock in scents and color and prevent further burning. Once the eggs have captured the desired color, place them back in the freezer.

Vacuum sealing eggs promotes a long shelf-life, and is a practice Thomas has employed for years.

1:2:3 Brine

INGREDIENTS
- 1/4 cup (1 Part) noniodized salt
- 1/2 cup (2 Parts) sugar
- 3/4 cup (3 Parts) borax
- 2 quarts of water

The second cure shared by Gary Thomas is one he likes when in a pinch. It's a fast cure that has yielded many fish for him over the years. He calls it his 1:2:3 cure.

Start by mixing the ingredients in water. In this ratio, it takes several minutes of intense stirring to dissolve most of the powders. In fact, the powders may not fully dissolve. Thomas likes a saturated solution, believing that once the eggs are added, frequent stirring will result in chemicals getting disturbed, thus more effectively penetrating the cells. Once the brine is stirred, place the eggs – already cut to desired bait sizes (or in skein strips) – into the cure. Gently stir the eggs every 15 minutes or so, to encourage proper mixture and absorption of the ingredients.

"When the mixture has been stirred a few times, you can experiment with scents," adds Thomas. "Though diffusion is taking place at this stage, adding the scents now will give them time to mix

The eggs from this cure retain their natural color extremely well.

with the fluids that will eventually be reabsorbed into the egg." At this point he will often add a 1/2 cup of Pautzke's Balls O' Fire Nectar to the brine. Thomas believes variations like this have paid off for him when other cures did not produce fish.

After 2 or 3 hours of soaking in the brine, remove the eggs and place them in a colander to let drain for 15-20 minutes. Thomas then suggests rinsing them under ice water to remove unwanted residues and stop the juicing process. If you want to firm up the baits, place them on paper towels and allow to air dry to a desired texture. At this stage, the eggs are ready to fish. Caution must be taken to watch this cure closely. The liberal amount of salt used acts fast on the eggs, pulling the contents through the membrane surprisingly quickly. The drying can be done at room temperature, or in a shaded, ventilated place outside. If dried outside, this step may take only a few minutes if the area is dry and airy.

For another twist to this cure, you can forgo the water, making it a fast – reacting dry cure. Simply add a packet of Jell-O for color. Raspberry is a popular flavor that yields good color. This dry-cure version does take longer than the water cure to set up, but not as long as other dry cures Thomas has used. The length of time depends on how hard you want the eggs and can be determined by touch. When done, either version of this cure can be frozen as described in the previous chapter.

Once on the river, Thomas may apply oils such as anise, shrimp, and anchovy to individual baits. "If a particular bait and oil combination is not producing and I believe fish are down there, I'll keep changing my approach in hopes of eliciting a bite," offers Thomas.

Gary Thomas and his son Rob (pictured here) have caught numerous salmon and steelhead on this cure.

Thomas's mind is always working. He's constantly experimenting with cures. "Sometimes the fish don't bite. I'm always wondering what I can do differently with my eggs that will tempt a bite," ponders Thomas. He marks all of his jars so he knows what cures he has in front of him at all times. Rarely will he take to the river without two or three different cures on hand.

"One day we fished Oregon's Coquille River for winter steelhead," Thomas reflects. "My buddy was having no luck on his cure, nor was I, so I switched eggs a couple of times. On the third cure I found what they wanted and we hit seven fish in one hole. It made me a believer in trying new things on the river, and only reconfirmed my theory that using different cures is critical to success."

Don't be afraid to test various cures and drift bobber combinations.

The Minds Behind the Cure

INGREDIENTS
  • Amerman Egg Cure

When it comes to acquiring fishing knowledge, being a guide has its advantages. Spending long, often intense hours in nature's classroom is the best medium in which to study and learn about the prey we seek. Approached with an open mind, a desire to constantly enlighten one's knowledge base, and a zest to master key elements of fishing, a student of the sport knows no limits. Perpetually hypothesizing and experimenting is what it's all about. Though results may be the reward of discrete examination, their impact may be eternal.

Scott Amerman is one such student of the sport. Scott stepped into a blessed life. His father, Gary Amerman, has been fishing professionally for more than 30 years and is one of the Pacific Northwest's most noted and successful guides. Now Scott is making his mark in the industry. Having fished since the age of five, Scott jump-started his guiding career in 1988 while still a teenager.

Scott and his father are two of the most successful egg fishermen around, and they have developed their own line of cured eggs and prepackaged cures. No, we are not going to reveal the ingredients that make Amerman's Eggs so effective, but we are going to look at what these men have done – and continue to do – to develop one of the most popular cured eggs in the fishing fraternity. In this chapter, Scott tells his approach to developing a quality cure.

Anglers often approach me, telling me how lucky I am to have had a father in the sport to do the legwork in developing such an effective cure. What few people realize is that we are constantly scrutinizing our cure. We are never content with where we are. Since I started guiding, we've changed our recipe three times. We are always keeping our minds open to new things and are constantly increasing our knowledge of the science behind fishing. Just because we have an effective product out there does not mean we will stop looking for ways to improve it. Every trip we make we pay close attention to river conditions, water temperature, environmental factors, the stages where fish may be in their migratory process and what minerals, chemicals, or pheromone stimulants these fish might be craving. These are just some of the factors behind developing a potent egg cure.

This mindset is one anglers looking to develop their own egg cure can adopt and benefit from. Spending 40-50 consecutive days, eight hours a day, up to 200 days a year on the river, fishing salmon eggs has given me an opportunity to thoroughly study salmon and steelhead. Whether salmon or steelhead fishing any day of the year, I fish salmon eggs. I don't troll, and I don't pull plugs. Egg fishing this many days a year, often fishing three or more rods, gives me a lot of hours spent studying fish and their reactions to eggs.

Though few people have the luxury of spending so much time on the water, you can still benefit from the time you do have. If your time is limited, try working with a group of friends and pool the knowledge you gain. If you don't have time to try all the cures in this book, start with a couple or start with a marketed cure and gain the benefits of others' research. Or go with a guide. You may learn more in one day than you can learn on your own all year. The more bits of information you can attain, the closer you come to piecing together all pieces of the egg-curing puzzle.

Let's look at what we know about salmon. Salmon have an incredible sense of smell. They can detect smells in parts per billion. This equates to filling 50 box cars with water, then adding two tablespoons of salt to one car. The smell of salt within the total volume of water will be detected by fish. Fish can smell the different mineral contents in rivers to know which ones to return to.

Amerman's cures turn out great looking, very effective eggs.

When a salmon enters fresh water, it's on its way to death. Salmon no longer can digest food and quickly lose the desire to feed. At the same time salmon quit feeding, their bodies go through vast physiological changes as their reproductive organs develop and steal their body's nutrients. This can lead to strong cravings for different minerals and nutrients. To better understand this correlation, think of it this way: A pregnant woman craves bizarre foods at various stages in her pregnancy. Why? Because her body is being depleted of nutrients and has certain needs for minerals and nutrients to help develop the baby. As this happens, her body starts craving strange foods that contain these minerals and nutrients. Since we know these fish are not eating but are having strong cravings, we know the easiest way to rekindle their strike instinct is to target these cravings.

Consider hunting. Everyone knows that deer and elk are drawn to salt. Why? Because it's something their body is craving, and it's hard for them to find in the wild. Hunters also utilize pheromones, such as male and female deer and elk urine or the scent of an in-heat female to attract their prey. We as fisherman can learn a lot from the hunting world.

When it comes to curing eggs for salmon fishing, I take what I know about salmon and break down my curing efforts for each of the three senses with which we can affect a salmon: smell, taste, and sight.

A salmon's sense of smell is very strong and easily its best sense. It is also the most important one to think about when curing eggs. A salmon will smell your bait long before it sees it. If the smell of the bait carries the right combination of stimulants, it will rekindle the strike instinct in a fish and make that fish search for the bait. A good salmon cure should produce a great deal of milking action on the eggs, filling the water around the bait with scent. This is easy to see when fishing, for when the eggs hit the water, there should be a cloud of scent leaving the bait, turning the water close to the eggs white. This is the scent trail the fish will follow to locate your bait.

Second, the eggs must taste good to a salmon. A good-tasting egg will be swallowed by a salmon, not mouthed. If fish aren't taking the bait deep into their mouths and upper stomach, it is not tasting good to them. Obviously the longer a fish holds onto the bait and the deeper it takes it into its mouth, the better chance we have of hooking it. I believe that a good-tasting cure will make a fish more aggressive towards a bait and make them come back time and time again, even when missed. I have fished some cures that have got the scent thing figured out and tend to get bitten a lot, but have yet to figure out the taste part. The bites I do get with these cures are usually missed as the fish don't take the bait well inside their mouth and never swallow them.

The last aspect of a good cure for fishing salmon is that it looks good. Eggs must be visually appealing. They must be capable of holding up cast after cast, and they must maintain color, even while quickly milking out. The look of the eggs will be the next step in how a fish finds your bait after smelling it. I consider dyes a key component in the curing process and devote a great deal of time to this single aspect. Finding the right color can have a major impact on your final outcome.

On one memorable trip, my dad, our clients, and I got into salmon in a deep hole. We were fishing eight bobbers with a variety of baits. The bite

Capturing the sight, smell and taste of a fish is what a prime egg cure is all about. Baits having good color and carrying scent into the water give anglers the edge.

started, but it was all on one bait. The bobbers with other baits fishing the same depth in the same water were being left alone. This continued for about 30 minutes with both boats landing fish, one after another, all on one bait. Then the bite slowed and one of the other bait bobbers went down. For the next 30 minutes the bait that had been red hot sat untouched, and the new flavor was the hot ticket. When the bite stopped on the second flavor, it started back up on the first. We hooked fish all day in this hole, as the fish went on and off the bite on different baits. The bite never stopped; the fish just preferred different baits at different times. This is a prime example of how a fish can undergo a change in appetite or at least a desire for certain minerals or scents. Most people would just assume the bite had ended or the fish had moved. The main difference in the cures we used was that one was working on mineral cravings and one had a pheromone stimulant.

You must have multiple baits on hand and be willing to use them when one doesn't produce. I have one cure I always use and take with me whenever I am on the river, but I take two or three others that I'm constantly experimenting with. For instance, if water temperatures rise, salmon may grow sluggish, thus requiring a different stimulant. Everyone knows that salmon live most of their lives in salt water and leave it when they start their spawning run. Most cures out there use some form of salt or sodium-based product knowing that fish will get a craving for salt. This is only one of the many cravings they will have; it is short lived, and it's the one craving that most everyone else is working on, too.

The secret to a great cure is having something that works along with everything else, but performs best when nothing else is working for anyone. I'd caution people not to get hung up on salt, sulfite, sulfide, nitrates, and nitrites in their cures. All are salt (sodium) derivatives, sharing comparable chemicals and reacting in similar ways within cures. I would encourage people to explore the other cravings fish have. Experiment with other minerals, chemicals, and pheromones. Most fishermen overlook the effective use of pheromones when it comes to revitalizing the aggressive tendencies and striking instincts of fish.

Steelhead are very different from salmon as are many of the techniques we use to fish for them. The metabolic and physiological changes steelhead go through are different from salmon. Steelhead are basically overgrown trout that have traveled to the ocean. These fish will survive spawning and their body changes happen much more slowly. Steelhead still carry a feeding instinct into the rivers, though it's debated as to whether or not they actually go on a feed. It's no secret they can and do aggressively pursue and strike food, or imitations thereof. This is why I focus my efforts on finding something steelhead like the taste of when targeting a cure for them. I consider taste to be the most important factor in fooling steelhead, followed by visual then olfactory senses.

Again, taste translates into how long they will hold onto the bait and how deep they will take it. Since these fish frequent fast water, you want a bait they won't hesitate holding on to once they strike it.

How many times have you fished a riffle where you cannot take the bow out of your line until the end of the drift? Having a bow in the line decreases its sensitivity, thus delaying the time from when the bite occurs to when you actually feel it, that is, if you feel it. Anyone who has fished steelhead by sight can relate to the need for developing a cure they will swallow. When sight-fishing for steelhead, it is common to drift a bait to a fish, then watch them pick it up and spit it out without ever having felt it. Steelhead are notorious for grabbing anything that goes by their nose, then spitting it back out if it doesn't taste good. Not until they take that bait into their mouth and hold on to it, will the bite be detected by feel.

A cure that has just the right color is also very important as the fish will decide whether or not to take it quickly based on the sight of the bait. Smell is far less important as the techniques used and the waters fished lead to less time for fish to stop and smell the eggs.

I don't believe steelhead carry the same mineral cravings as salmon, because their bodies do not undergo the same physical changes. This point reveals why many anglers shy away from mineral-based cures containing sulfites, sulfates, nitrates and iodized salt-based cures. Whatever ingredients you experiment with in your steelhead cures, be careful not to put the wrong sensory enhancers out there.

The Amerman's currently have two different egg cures on the market: one for salmon, one for steelhead. Each cure comes in two colors. They also market cured, packaged eggs prepared in these recipes. I advise always wearing rubber gloves to mask human scent and other odors that may be transmitted, as well as preventing dyes and harsh chemicals from penetrating your skin; a safety measure we should all take into consideration.

Though the Amerman's egg-curing ingredients may forever remain a secret, don't feel bad. Not even their wives and children know what goes into the magic potion, and I'm not sure they want to. Perhaps what's just as important, you are now more familiar with the mindset that goes into the creation of these cures. By utilizing the details presented in this chapter and applying them to the salmon, steelhead and rivers you fish, maybe you'll be the one to harbor a secret cure the rest of the fishing world will yearn to know.

Simple, Yet Effective

INGREDIENTS

- 1 cup powdered borax (heaping full)
- 1/4 cup white table sugar
- 1 box Jell-O

Pedaling his bike down the old gravel road, Dan Likens, routinely fished Oregon's Alsea River. Not yet old enough to drive, his biggest concern was catching a ride back home at dark, so he didn't have to pump his already fatigued legs.

That was in the mid-1950s. Today, the Alsea remains Likens' favorite river, though the road to his honey hole is now paved. At an early age, Likens had a zest for fishing, and over the years he's pursued salmon and steelhead all over Oregon.

The cure he uses today is one he picked up in 1967. At this time, borax was the primary "cure" used by most anglers. But somewhere along the line, dried, dark eggs spurred someone to add color to the recipe. One of the first times Liken tried this cure, he hooked 14 summer steelhead on a single trip. Ever since that day, he's been hooked. Over the past 30 years, Likens has had good success with this simple, clean cure.

Borax, sugar and Jell-O are all that's needed for Dan Likens' favorite egg cure. He's used this recipe for years and taken many steelhead on it.

With eggs already cut to bait size, spread them out on paper towels on top of a few layers of newspaper. Thoroughly mix all ingredients in a bowl and generously sprinkle over the eggs. Let the eggs sit at room temperature for 24 hours, rotating them from time to time.

After 24 hours, you can either package them up as is, or rinse them off to remove the hardened crust. If you choose to rinse them, place them back on paper towels and allow to air dry until a light crust forms on the eggs.

The beauty of this cure is its flexibility. You don't have to freeze this cure. Once the eggs are set, Likens has kept them in the refrigerator for up to four years, in only a jar or Ziploc bag.

If you want to prolong the shelf life of the eggs, place them in a vacuum-sealed bag or jar. If you don't have a vacuum – sealer, Likens says not to worry. Typically, he'll place the eggs in a canning jar, strike a match, stick it in the jar and quickly screw the lid back on. Eventually the flame will use up all the oxygen and fizzle out, vacuum sealing the container without the use of spendy machinery. Applying this method, Likens has kept vacuum-sealed eggs up to six years.

When in a pinch, the eggs can simply be bagged at the end of the 24-hour drying period and rinsed off when you go to use them on the river. After all, you may want the eggs hard and crusted if you're fishing fast water. "I'll get them pretty wet, removing all the crust if I'm fishing with bobbers," Likens claims. "I'll only get four or five casts from these soft baits, but their color holds well, thanks to the Jell-O."

Strawberry, raspberry, cherry and orange Jell-O all are solid color choices. I've even heard of guys using green. The choice is yours.

Lighting a match, placing it in the jar and quickly closing the lid eats up the oxygen, prolonging the shelf-life of cured eggs.

"As for the sugar, it's nothing more than a hardener," says Likens. "I'll use a bit more of it when I'm curing coho or chinook eggs because they seem to have more moisture in them. I've even heard of guys substituting salt for sugar in this recipe. While the sugar firms the eggs by forming a crusted layer on the outside, salt extracts moisture, toughening them up."

Not only is Likens an ardent angler, but he was a devoted coach and teacher most of his life. He worked at a few small schools around Oregon until 1968, when he laid down roots in Junction City. Today he's retired and continues to hammer astounding numbers of fish in many of the state's coastal streams.

Eternal Waters

INGREDIENTS

- Two 6 ounce cans of Fruit Fresh or Ever Fresh
- 1 cup borax
- 2 cups noniodized salt
- 1 fluid ounce red food coloring

The cures in the next two chapters were passed on to me by good friend, Scot Johnson of Walterville, Oregon. Johnson is one of the most dedicated outdoorsman I know. Born 100 years too late, Johnson is the type of man who is happiest with his gun in one hand, fishing rod in the other and a pack full of traps on his back, heading into the wilderness for an indefinite period of time.

As with most devoted outdoorsmen, Johnson does all he can to succeed in the wilderness, be it competing against the forces of nature, or man himself. The cures he shares are ones he's worked with for many years and both have been utilized by guides and avid anglers throughout the Pacific Northwest. In fact, there are some guides who rely on Johnson to cure their eggs for them.

This first recipe is simple, yet intriguing. Mix two, 6-ounce cans of Fruit Fresh or Ever Fresh, 1 cup borax and 2 cups noniodized salt into a glass one-gallon jar. Johnson prefers glass as it does not break down and give off any scent or film. Because this cure can sit wet for years, storage in a sturdy, glass jar is preferred over plastics.

With the dry ingredients thoroughly mixed, add your skeins of eggs. It doesn't matter if you have one or ten skeins, put them all in the jar, whole. Now fill the jar with water and add one fluid ounce of red food coloring. Mix around and let stand. Within 24 hours they are ready to fish.

The eggs stay in water, refrigerated, until they are ready to be used. "I have eggs in my shop refrigerator right

One of Scot Johnson's favorite cures requires sensible ingredients that work well.

now that have been sitting in this brine for over three years," smiles Johnson. "If I wanted to go fishing tomorrow, I wouldn't hesitate grabbing a skein from a jar and taking off. They're incredible eggs!"

Fruit Fresh or Ever Fresh can be purchased at any grocery store. These are intended to keep fruits and vegetables from browning and protect the flavor, preserving color loss and lengthening longevity. It works well on eggs, too. Even after years in this brine, the eggs are surprisingly sprite and succulent looking when this preservative is used.

"Some guides who use these eggs will remove the skeins from the jar the night prior to fishing," says Johnson. "They'll let them air-dry overnight to toughen 'em up a bit." Johnson notes that the eggs are messy to handle, and some people prefer wearing rubber gloves when cutting the baits to desired sizes and placing them on the hook.

Eggs can be left in, removed from or added to this curing solution at any point, over many years.

One of the reasons this cure is so popular is the eggs take a long time to milk out. The food coloring stays locked in the eggs and the Fruit Fresh helps hold it in. In fact, guys I spoke with who have used this cure like it because they can actually see the scents being released from the eggs over repeated casts, not just the first few throws.

Skeins can be added to this cure at any time. "Say you initially place two skeins in the cure. If you catch a hen the next day, toss her skeins in, too. If you catch another hen a month or two later, throw those skeins in. It doesn't matter when you add eggs to this brine, that's the beauty of it," remarks Johnson.

All eggs cure up well in this recipe, be it coho, spring or fall chinook, summer or winter steelhead. In addition, curing the entire skein at once and storing them for long time periods allows you to cut the baits to a desired size – small baits for summer steelhead in fast water, large baits for fall chinook.

Salt & Bricks

INGREDIENTS
- 4 cups borax
- 1 cup noniodized salt

The second cure used by Johnson is a favorite among steelhead anglers from the Willamette Valley to Idaho. It takes a lot of effort to pull this one off, but in the end you're rewarded with a solid egg that will likely outlast any natural cluster you've ever looped on to your hook.

In a dry area at room temperature, thoroughly mix four cups of borax and one cup of noniodized salt. This cure does not seem to work in cool settings or in areas of high humidity. Next, spread out several layers of newspaper. You'll want these layers to be thick, as they'll be absorbing drained juices for a couple days.

Now, pour the dry cure on the newspaper. One at a time, lay the skeins on the bed of cure and gently massage the brine into every nook and cranny in the eggs. Hit all the crevices and folds in the skein, making sure to open it up and work the brine into all areas.

Now take a piece of laminated wood or an extra piece of formica-finished counter top – something that's smooth and will not absorb any moisture. A small piece of wood is all you need, something to cover the skeins of eggs. Lay the board on top of the eggs, and place bricks on top of the wood. If curing two skeins, Johnson likes using two bricks. Three skeins, three bricks, and so on. Some larger firm skeins may require additional bricks be

A simple cure with an impressive outcome. It is pressure from bricks that makes these eggs set up so well.

added. You want enough weight so as to slowly compress the eggs without bursting the cell walls.

Let them sit for 12 hours, then remove the bricks and board. With a soft, four-inch bristled paintbrush, it's time to tediously whisk away the cure from all parts of the skeins. Throw away all of the used cure and lay down fresh newspaper.

With the old curing ingredients gone, mix another four cups of borax and one cup noniodized salt. Repeat the entire process as described above, but with the opposite side of the skeins facing down. Repeat this process two more times, rotating the skeins each time, adding fresh brine every time and adding or changing newspaper if necessary.

The end result is a very firm skein that's about a 1/2 inch thick. If the skeins are an inch or more thick, you'll want to carry out another step to flatten and harden the eggs a bit more. When completed, you should be able to hold a corner of the skein and not have the remainder of the skein collapse, it's that stiff. The eggs maintain their natural color with this recipe without the presence of additives. In the water they hold their bright orange color amazingly well and for extended periods.

When heading to the river, Johnson either cuts several 1/2" x 1/2" cubes to take with him, or cuts them in the field. Until it comes time to cut them, this is a very clean cure to work with. When you do cut them, juices that are under pressure will be released and it can get a bit messy if you're not careful.

When storing the eggs from this cure, refrigeration is not necessary. Keeping them at room temperature or in a cool shop works just fine.

"These baits are nearly indestructible. They stay on so long you'll get tired of them and want to change for simple peace of mind. But the steelhead whack 'em in fast water," concludes Johnson.

While on the subject of noniodized salt, I recently spoke with a guide who, when low on eggs, carries salt with him in the boat. As soon as a client catches a hen, he removes the skeins, cuts them to bait size, lays them on a towel and covers them with salt. In no time, moisture is pulled from the eggs,

These salmon skeins cured up well. The salt cure creates a tough egg that maintains its natural color very well.

they firm up and with their natural color locked in, are ready to fish. He's taken many fall chinook and winter steelhead using this emergency salt cure.

A Quick Cure

INGREDIENTS
- Quick Cure
- Noniodized salt
- Optional oils and scents

February, 2001, Oregon guide Bret Stuart and his clients boated 180 winter steelhead. That same year, he absolutely clobbered the summer steelhead. Stuart is best known for his jig fishing, crafting what many seasoned anglers claim to be the best steelhead jig ever made. But, as with other fishing tactics, jigs don't produce 100% of the time. When not using jigs, Stuart relies on eggs as the next best thing.

Like most guides, Stuart is pressed for time during the height of salmon and steelhead season. Because he personally hand-creates his own jigs and markets them throughout the West, Stuart's time is precious. For this reason, Stuart relies on a quick, easy cure that produces fish and allows him flexibility in his schedule to tend other matters.

Quick Cure and scents are a favorite combination for Oregon guide, Bret Stuart.

Stuart's favorite cure is simple. All that's needed is a package of Quick Cure. Like many packaged egg cures now on the market, Quick Cure has all the ingredients, ready to go. Created by Cure-Rite Products out of Tillamook, Oregon, Quick Cure comes in a variety of colors and is usually available through local tackle shops.

After cleaning his eggs of all blood residue, Stuart blots them dry with a paper towel. He then takes a whole skein and places it in a gallon-size Ziploc bag. With one hand he cradles the skein – membrane side down in the palm of the hand – and works his thumb into the folds of the eggs. With the other hand, he sprinkles Quick Cure over the exposed eggs.

Stuart works with both hands in the bag, so any spilled cure ends up in the bottom. Ensuring every crevice within the skein is lightly covered in Quick Cure, he repeats the same steps on the second skein. He will work up to four skeins per bag.

Once the eggs are covered in Quick Cure, Stuart closes the bag and works any excess powder into the skein by gently rolling them around. He then places the bag of eggs on its side in his garage. They sit in this position overnight, creating their own juice.

Before heading to work the next morning, Stuart flips the bag over, so the opposite side of the eggs are face down. In this

Thoroughly rubbing the cure into every crevice in the skein is critical to obtaining a quality berry.

position, the eggs reabsorb the juices they created, better preserving them while at the same time locking in color and scent.

Upon returning home at the end of the work day, stuart simply cuts the baits into desired sizes and places them in baggies. Twenty four hours from the time he begins, the eggs are ready to fish, refrigerate, or stick in the freezer. I've talked with guys who use the same cure and they have kept eggs in the refrigerator, soaking in their own juices, for up to a year.

Stuart prefers the fluorescent red Quick Cure; he feels it gives him deeper, longer-lasting hues that fish desire. It should be noted, the amount of Quick Cure you use determines the firmness of the eggs. If you desire a firm egg, use more Quick Cure. For softer eggs, apply smaller portions of the cure.

If, when fishing with a baggy of eggs, they begin to juice, Stuart sprinkles noniodized salt on the clusters to toughen them up a bit. This prolongs the life of the eggs and better controls the milking process by causing plasmolysis to occur at a slower rate.

Once the baits are ready to fish, Stuart applies the scents. For salmon, he prefers the liquid form of Salmon Feast Smelly Jelly, produced by the Catcher Company of Hillsboro, Oregon. He also has good results with Pautzke's Balls O' Fire Nectar. Once the cluster is in his egg loop, Stuart adds a drop of either the Smelly Jelly or Nectar directly to the eggs. If, after several casts, the eggs need freshening, simply add another drop of oil or scent.

Another trick that's rapidly catching on is marinading cured eggs in liquid Smelly Jelly. Once the eggs are cured, place them in a Ziploc bag and douse with the liquid form of Smelly Jelly in your scent of choice. Let sit for two or three days in the refrigerator, allowing time for the scents to permeate the eggs.

Adding scents during or after the curing process is something Stuart experiments with to a great extent.

For his steelhead eggs, Stuart favors the jelly form of shrimp with anise Smelly Jelly. When applying the jelly version, he puts the bait on his hook, then dips it into the container, smearing the jelly onto the eggs. This is Stuart's preferred method of fishing his eggs when spotting steelies and casting to them, as you can actually watch the fish react to scent.

One summer day I fished with Stuart. A nice steelie laid at the head of a riffle and we threw everything we had at him. Despite having an arsenal dangled on his nose, the fish never made an attempt to even open his mouth. Then Stuart dipped a fresh cluster of eggs in his jar of Smelly Jelly. The next cast, Stuart anchored the bait two inches from the nose of the fish. The presentation was too irresistible and at long last, the finicky fish blasted out of the river and made a pair of impressive runs before I slipped the net beneath his silver belly.

Stuart lives near Oregon's McKenzie River, but travels the state in search of salmon, steelhead, and trout. To learn more about Stuart's 24/7 Guide Service and his famous Steelhead Bullet Jigs, refer to the appendix.

Stuart with a winter steelhead taken on the cure described here.

Pro-Cure:
Creativity & An Open Mind

Suffering a major setback did not keep Pro-Cure from getting their production line back on track.

A book on egg cures would not be complete without the inclusion of Pro-Cure, the first commercial cure to hit the market. While we won't go into detail on the ingredients in Pro-Cure, we will look at the thought process that goes into developing several Pro-Cure products.

Phil Pirone, president and originator of Pro-Cure, followed his heart. Growing up in New York and New Jersey, Pirone took to fly fishing in his youth. Wanting to escape the crowds, he packed up and moved to Oregon in 1977. He ran a fly shop in Eugene, eventually getting into the guiding business. His guiding ventures took him throughout Oregon and Alaska.

Pirone was fortunate to work with expert guide Denny Hannah, who introduced him to a sulfite cure. "We talked about dying eggs different colors and began experimenting around with it," smiles Pirone. "We eventually got some great-looking eggs by combining sulfites and red dyes. These baits were hot. We were pulling salmon from under peoples' noses, the same people who claimed a bright-red egg would never work on chinook."

"Salmon are chemical junkies, and I tested cures with that in mind. Whenever I went out on the river, guys would ask to use my eggs. I gladly shared with them, for I wanted everyone to catch fish. Then someone commented that I should market the recipe since it worked so well. I looked into going commercial, but all the advice I received indicated there was no market, and to sell my idea to a fishing company already in place would be the wise thing to do."

With a lifetime of fishing experience behind him, Pirone had a great deal of faith in his newly developed cure, and listened to no one's

Pro-Cure has a complete line of egg curing and handling components.

recommendation. By 1984 his Pro-Cure company was in full-swing. Today, some 20 employees work at Pro-Cure, curing, mixing, testing, and shipping products worldwide. There's also an extensive line of guides, writers, professional lecturers, and experts in the field who are constantly testing each and every product and reporting their finds.

Though Pro-Cure suffered a big setback during the September, 2001 fire that destroyed their plant, they are back up and running at a new location.

In talking with Pirone about eggs and cures, he brought up some very interesting points, points he considers vital and which he adheres to when working with any of his products.

"People need to keep an open mind," stated Pirone when asked what anglers can do to catch more salmon and steelhead on cured eggs. "These fish are not smart, we just have to keep trying new things until we find what they like."

Pirone believes the key to a good cure is one that locks in color. He points out how dyes are crucial to the curing process, not only because they give good color to the eggs, but because they give anglers confidence. "If you have confidence in something, you're more likely to use it. This is how we learn what fish like," he states.

Take Pro-Cure's Slam-Ola powder. The company discovered a need for a new cure and thought the ingredients in Slam-Ola would hold the answer. The more they worked with it, the more they learned it didn't work as a cure. It did however fill a niche of a much-needed additive, and is one of the most productive, hottest-selling Pro-Cure products on the market.

Pirone shed light on another interesting fact, and if you think about the science behind his reasoning, it makes sense. "Having to wait to cure your eggs (once you've caught a fish and removed the eggs) is not necessarily a bad thing," he shared with me. He used to think otherwise, until he cured some foul-smelling eggs himself.

"While it works great on fresh roe, your eggs are smelling bad, brining them will take some of the smell out by removing fats. Think about flushing

Phil Pirone, President of Pro-Cure, tests the potency of scents he's working with in the lab.

Pro-Cured eggs being set to dry prior to wrapping and being sent to the market. Note the plastic screens on which the eggs sit, so as to avoid contact with the galvanized mesh below.

a wound on your leg. It's more thorough to flush a wound with a solution that removes the bacteria than it is to cover it with a powder. Brining tainted eggs opens them up, allowing cures and dyes to permeate the entire part of the egg. All the fats and bacteria rise to the top of the brine, leaving a quality egg. But you have to work with a 100% salt brine. Not only will this produce cleaner eggs, it will yield brighter colors than sprinkling on a dry cure would."

In putting together this book, I personally tested every cure. When a buddy passed along some pungent eggs to me, I had to give Pirone's theory a try. The eggs came out nearly odor free, and with the addition of scents and oils, you would have never known they were tainted from the start. Two days later, my dad caught a winter steelhead on these eggs. The moral of the story: don't toss those foul-smelling eggs, they might be salvageable.

Pirone also advocates people experimenting with extremes in the way of scents and attractants. He'll play around with anything. He recently injected chocolate syrup into his plug-cut herring. He caught two nice silvers, one right after the other. He never touched a fish again on that combination. But it's what initially happened, what caused those fish to strike in the first place that drives Pirone nuts.

"There was something in there that triggered a bite. I'm always experimenting trying to figure it out. I'm currently working with watermelon extract, before that it was root beer. Root beer was a carrier smell I once detected in a scent. If it works as a carrier, why not as a primary attractant?

Fish love sweet stuff, this is why eggs covered in clover honey turn out to be so productive. I'm always working with sweets and trying new things."

Pirone has also experimented with vanilla extract, an ingredient found in WD-40. Liquid smoke, squid scents, oils, and numerous other attractants have been put to use at one time or another, and most have produced. "The more diversified the scents and cures you fish, the better your odds of finding what fish like. If they bite something, it's not by accident, there was something there that triggered that bite. It might not work again that day, or the next, but hang on to it, it will produce down the road."

Natural bait scents are another source Pirone encourages anglers to factor in when curing eggs. "One-third of what steelhead eat in the ocean are squid, yet few people use this attractant for them. And, given the vast number of sardines off the Oregon Coast in recent years, this is a major portion of their diet as well. Then there's crawfish, a natural enemy of steelhead and salmon, that destroy their redds. Fish have been known to kill crawdads on sight. Given these facts, why not throw the fish a banana split, like garlic – scented crawdads?"

The point Pirone brings up is a good one. Why not mix all these scents together and try that on your egg cures. Better yet, cure one batch of eggs with sardine scents, another with squid, and a third with crawfish. Then make the fourth cure the "banana split." Such an arsenal will present variety, a factor Pirone sees as crucial, stating how fish tend not to react to a bait they see repeatedly or smell in front of their noses.

When asked about applying scents to egg cures, Pirone made clear that to his knowledge, there are no miracle scents out there. He believes scents alone won't come close to catching salmon and steelhead, but considers them to be a key piece in the entire puzzle.

"Trust your nose," he advised when asked about scents. "If you have to struggle to detect smells in a bottle of scent, why even add it to your cure?"

By applying Pirone's fanatical mindset of trying virtually anything and everything you believe will attract fish, you may experience an increased success rate. Wavering from the ruts and routines we often find ourselves caught in, think of the undiscovered world of fishing that awaits trial. By going to the extremes in your egg-curing tests, you may discover more than you bargained for. And if you think it's all been done before, think again.

From a man who makes a living knowing salmon, steelhead, their eggs, and scents that catch these fish, Pirone sums it up in one sentence.

"As humans, we think we have all the answers, when, in reality we know very little about salmon and steelhead."

With that attitude, Pirone knows no limits, which is why Pro-Cure has been a world leader in cures and scents for nearly 20 years. There's no reason every angler can't adopt this vision and put it to use, starting now.

Saltwater Brine

INGREDIENTS

- Noniodized salt
- Orange Jell-O
- Borax
- Beau Mac Instant Bait Coloring
- Pro-Cure Bait Cure Redd Hot Double Stuff

A man who has spent a lifetime on one of Oregon's most famed salmon and steelhead streams is Doug Coplin. Coplin taught and retired from Glide High School, situated along the banks of the North Umpqua River. For decades he's experimented with cures, including some recipes he acquired from local legends. Over the years, he's conversed with hundreds of anglers on recipes and their theories behind them. Now that he's retired, he systematically tinkers with cures, but the one he considers among the most effective, both in looks and productivity, is a saltwater cure.

When curing eggs for steelhead fishing, begin the process by stirring noniodized salt into a plastic or glass container of cool tap water. Use enough water to cover the amount of eggs you want to cure. Pour in some salt and mix thoroughly. Continue adding and mixing salt until you reach the point of saturation, where the salt no longer dissolves.

If working with small skeins, place them in the brine, whole. If curing medium-sized skeins, you can cut them in half, lengthwise down the middle. For mature chinook eggs with excessively large skeins, cut them into manageable strips, ensuring enough membrane remains intact with the eggs to hold together. Place the strips, or skeins, of eggs into the saltwater brine.

You'll know you have enough salt when the eggs float. If the eggs don't float, or at least suspend in the water, remove them and stir the brine more thoroughly, adding more salt if necessary. Once the eggs are placed in the brine, soak them for one hour.

Using enough salt to send the eggs afloat is critical in acquiring a quality cure from this brine.

At the end of one hour, remove the eggs and cut to the desired bait size. Placing them on a couple layers of white, unscented paper towels, allow them time to dry, or blot them dry until they are slightly tacky to the touch. While the baits are drying, mix one part orange Jell-O to three parts borax into a bowl or onto paper towels. Take the baits and roll them in the powder mixture until they are completely covered. Then place them on white paper towels, allowing them to air-dry to your desired texture. At this point they are ready to fish or freeze. Eggs cured in this manner freeze very well and last a long time when fished, milking out very well.

Coplin adds, if the baits turn out too dry for your liking, leave the clusters in larger pieces when rolling them in the Jell-O/borax mixture. He's

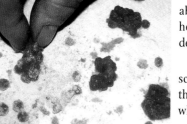

had good results curing eggs about six times the bait size he uses, cutting them to desired size once on the river.

If you wish to add liquid scents, the ideal time is after they've been rolled in powder, while they are air drying. On

Thoroughly roll the air-dried baits in the borax/Jell-O mixture, then let harden to desired texture.

some batches, Coplin sprays WD-40, which he especially likes for salmon. He also applies liberal amounts of WD-40 to his hands while in the boat and handling baits when salmon fishing.

Coplin has been using WD-40 on eggs since the early 1970s. He especially likes it on this cure when fishing salmon.

When applying this egg recipe for salmon fishing, Coplin follows the same procedure, but substitutes two key ingredients. He likes these eggs to carry more red coloration, so adds Beau Mac's Instant Bait Coloring to his saltwater brine. When the eggs are soaking in the brine, they absorb the red coloring, enhancing the hue of the finished product. He then removes the eggs, cuts them to bait size and blots them dry or allows them time to air-dry. Once sticky-dry, he rolls them in Pro-Cure Bait Cure Redd Hot Double Stuff instead of the Jell-O and borax mix. Allowing the red baits ample time to firm up, they are then ready to fish, refrigerate, or freeze.

"The advantage of a salt brine is that it toughens the membranes really well," offers Coplin. In the rushing waters of the North and South Umpqua – along with several other Cascade-born rivers Coplin fishes – a tough egg that withstands raging turbidity, boulder strewn bottoms and bedrock ledges is a must. The saltwater sets the eggs to a point they withstand a great deal of punishment, and they catch fish. In fact, the day prior to sharing this recipe, Coplin and his buddy hooked 13 winter steelhead and boated ten using eggs from this cure.

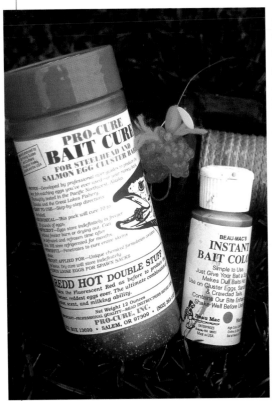

"Another advantage of this cure is how great it works on frozen eggs," Coplin adds. "I get a lot of silver salmon eggs from Alaska and they arrive at my home frozen. Not until I used this recipe was I happy with the way raw, frozen eggs cured up. This is the best recipe I've found for treating frozen eggs because the saltwater toughens up the membranes of the already weakened eggs. This fact alone has allowed me to retain a greater number of eggs to use in all of my salmon and steelhead fishing."

For anglers who run short on eggs and have to purchase frozen skeins, give this cure a try. I personally applied it to frozen silver salmon eggs. I can promise, you won't be disappointed with the results.

When curing eggs for salmon fishing, Coplin prefers substituting Pro-Cure's Redd Hot Double Stuff and Beau Mac's Instant Bait Coloring for the borax and Jell-O. Doing so creates a deep red berry that drives salmon crazy.

Bit-O-Honey

INGREDIENTS

- Clover honey
- Sodium sulfite

Doug Coplin shared so many unique and interesting cures with me, it was tough narrowing down the field of which ones to include. But the good ol' honey cure had to be part of this recipe collection.

Years ago Coplin borrowed this cure from a friend and has used it ever since. Along with the previous recipe, this is one he uses quite extensively. He especially likes it for chinook salmon.

Begin by taking a plastic jar or container that's large enough to house the quantity of eggs you're going to cure. Taking ten white paper towels, stack them atop one another, turn the curing jar upside down and trace around the mouth of it. Then cut the circles out. These circles must fit inside the curing jar.

Doug Coplin considers this one of his most coveted recipes. The natural sugars found in honey can be especially appealing to a fishes sense of smell.

Place five of the paper towels in the bottom of the jar, saving the other half for the top layer.

With the paper towels in place, cut your eggs to the desired bait size and place a layer on the bottom of the jar. Sprinkle a light layering of sodium sulfite over the eggs. Then lightly drip honey onto the sulfite-covered eggs, just enough to get a gloss. It's not critical to get honey on every bait, for the steps will be repeated several times.

Lay down another layer of eggs and repeat the sodium-sulfite sprinkling and honey-dripping steps. Do this until all of the baits have been utilized. As the honey runs over and through the baits, it will disperse throughout the jar, penetrating all the eggs.

The honey contains natural sugars that salmon find irresistible. The sulfite, as in all cures in which it's used, acts as a preservative and greatly enhances the juicing of eggs.

With the final layer of eggs dusted in sulfite and lightly covered in honey, place the remaining five layers of paper towels on top. The paper towels serve to absorb any excess moisture that's created. Screw the lid securely on and place in a cool setting. If it's too warm outside or in the garage, Coplin likes placing the container in the refrigerator. It takes two days for this cure to fully set up.

There is no need to invert the jar in this cure, as the viscous honey takes a long time to precipitate through the eggs. At the end of two days – you can

Once sodium sulfite has been sprinkled on the eggs, apply a thin coating of honey.

even extend it to a third day – remove the eggs and place in small containers or baggies. Coplin likes storing these eggs in the refrigerator, where they will keep for several months. The eggs from this cure maintain their natural colors and milk out very well.

Impressed by the number and diversity of recipes that Coplin offered me, I had to meet this guy in person. We fished together on Oregon's North Umpqua River, and even got into some fish. But what really struck me was Coplin's attitude toward the sport of fishing.

"Some fishermen may be offended by my sharing the deep dark secrets found in these cures, but I could never figure out why fishermen are so worried about helping out a fellow angler. Everyone has to learn somehow, either through someone else or through their own trial and error. I truly love to fish and hunt and I feel good about sharing information that may help others find a little more success," Coplin mused.

Doug Coplin lives on the banks of one of Oregon's premier rivers. He catches more fish in a season than many anglers take in a lifetime.

Brown Sugar on the Rogue

INGREDIENTS

- 2 cups brown sugar
- 1 cup white sugar
- 4 cups water
- Borax

Brown sugar cures have been around for many years, yet fewer and fewer people appear to be using them. Sugars, be it brown or white, act as hardeners. But it's the sweet aroma they give off, many anglers believe, that makes them so effective. By combining brown and white sugar, smells are introduced into the river that fish, especially salmon, find appealing.

In this chapter we will look at two cures in which brown sugar is the key ingredient. Both cures came from the Rogue River, one of the West Coast's top salmon streams.

Buzz Ramsey acquired this recipe in the early 1970s. At the time, it was one of the more popular cures on the Rogue, and it still produces fish.

The first recipe is a water cure that was shared by Buzz Ramsey. Buzz was turned on to this technique back in 1972. "Though it's a little homespun, this cure catches fish," offers Buzz. That's all we need to know.

Mix two cups brown sugar and one cup white sugar into four cups of water, stirring until the sugars have dissolved. Then cut your skeins into bait-size pieces and soak in the solution overnight, or for about 12 hours.

Remove the eggs from the brine and let the excess water drain off. Place the eggs on white paper towels or drying racks and allow to air-dry for two hours.

The eggs are now ready to fish. If you intend on freezing the baits, first pack them in borax. Cover the eggs with enough borax to prevent them from sticking together. Eggs cured in this manner are best if used within 90 days, but will keep for up to a year in the freezer.

INGREDIENTS
- 1 Cup brown sugar
- 1 teaspoon sodium sulfite

The second brown sugar recipe also has its roots on the Rogue River and is another cure that Doug Coplin likes for fishing salmon. Doug has used this dry cure on both spring and fall chinook in several Oregon rivers with good success. He first learned of this cure back in 1965, when brown sugar cures were very popular.

Begin by combining one cup brown sugar and a teaspoon of sodium sulfite. Mix the two ingredients into a jar or large shaker, as both will be simultaneously added to the eggs.

Taking a medium-size glass or plastic jar, one that peanut butter or mayonnaise comes in, layer the bottom with bait-size chunks of eggs.

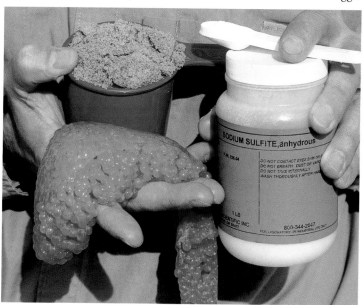

Doug Coplin picked this cure up on the Rogue, back in 1965.

Sprinkle a generous layer of the powder mixture over the eggs. Apply enough powder to lightly cover the eggs, but don't smother them.

Add another layer of eggs and apply the cure, repeating this process until all the eggs have been used. Tightly secure the lid and let sit for about twelve hours, or overnight. At this time, invert the jar and let sit 12 more hours. Then invert one more time, again letting sit 12 hours.

Though it's a time-consuming process, requiring 36 hours, the tipping is necessary to allow the juices time to seep down through the eggs, absorbing into the cells. The brown sugar and sodium sulfite draw quite a bit of moisture from the eggs and the inverting of the jar allows these juices, along with the chemicals, time to be reabsorbed.

"These eggs turn out very natural in color, and milk extremely well, releasing lots of scent into the water," Coplin adds, which is one reason he likes them so much. The finished product turns out soupy, and may be drained if too much juice has accumulated. But keep the eggs soupy, don't air-dry them, advises Coplin, as that's a key quality you want to retain from this cure, especially when fishing salmon in deep water.

Coplin has learned that eggs from this cure do not freeze well. Instead, he stores them in a refrigerator, where they will easily keep for three months.

Big fish like big baits. This 70 pound chinook took a monster bait. Here a size 0 Spin-N-Glo shows just how big the bait truly is.

Great Lakes Combo

INGREDIENTS

- 1 cup borax
- 1/2 cup sugar, or cherry or orange Jell-O
- 1 cup noniodized salt

David Keene is a building contractor residing north of Detroit, Michigan. He guided professionally for a decade, but has been fishing salmon and steelhead for nearly 30 years. Keene is an ambassador for Pure Fishing, a conglomerate of many fishing-related companies, thus he is constantly on the water testing products and putting proven ones to use.

Keene provides two of his favorite cures in this chapter. The first is a cluster cure he's had great success with in his home waters. The second is a single-egg cure.

When curing egg clusters from the Great Lakes region, David Keene advises utilizing river running fish whose eggs are firmer than those found in the Lakes.

Keene has found this first cure to be very productive on salmon, especially when backbouncing. He's also had good success catching brown trout on this cure.

Keene starts with a good skein of eggs, ones derived from river fish. "Curing eggs from salmon caught in the Great Lakes is tough," Keene offers. "Their eggs just seem too mushy and full of water. They don't set up well, which is why I like getting river-run salmon eggs for this recipe."

Upon catching a hen, Keene immediately removes the eggs and places them on ice in the cooler. He does not rinse them off, and prefers to begin the curing process within 24 to 48 hours.

Begin by mixing borax, sugar, and salt into a bowl or baggie for this powder cure. If you wish to add color to your eggs, you can substitute Jell-O for the sugar. If it's red eggs you desire, substitute one box of cherry Jell-O. If it's orange eggs you want, substitute one box of orange Jell-O. If the natural color is what you wish to preserve, stay with the white sugar.

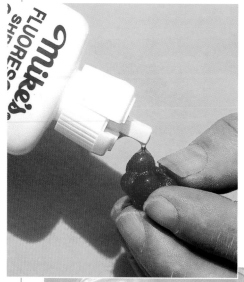

Adding scents to his cured eggs is something Keene routinely tests.

Take the fresh skeins and pat dry with a paper towel or allow time to air-dry on the towels for one or two hours. In humid regions, Keene prefers placing the eggs on paper towels and putting a fan on them to dry them out a bit. He has even placed them directly on cookie sheets, elevating one end to allow moisture to drain from the eggs. Once tacky to the touch, fillet the skeins lengthwise, ensuring ample membrane stays intact. Then cut to desired bait sizes.

Roll the egg clusters around in the cure, making sure all parts get covered. If curing big baits, Keene advises taking pinches of the cure and working it into the folds of each bait. Once covered, begin placing the eggs into a glass jar or plastic container. When the container is 1/4 the way full of eggs, sprinkle a generous layer of cure over top. Repeat this again at the 1/2, 3/4, and full points.

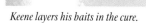

Keene layers his baits in the cure.

Seal the top of the container and refrigerate. Keene has fished eggs from this recipe that were stored in his refrigerator for six years, and they looked and performed great. He does warn though, if curing eggs from Great Lakes salmon, they only seem to last a maximum of six months in the refrigerator. There's no need to freeze eggs cured this way.

Keene does like storing these eggs in small containers, something he'd use up in one day's fishing. Because the humidity level is so high in his part of the country, Keene advises against storing eggs after they've been exposed to the elements.

In recent years, Keene has been experimenting with oils and scents in this cure. He's used many of Atlas-Mike's products, and is especially fond of their spawn scent. When on the river, he'll apply two or three drops of the scent to his bait. He likes the way the scent milks out in the water and believes this has improved his success.

INGREDIENTS
- 2 tablespoons boric acid
- 1 tablespoon white sugar
- 2 tablespoons sodium sulfate
- 1 quart water

Many salmon and steelhead taken in Keene's region of the country are mature specimens whose eggs are often loose when the fish are caught. This is one reason single egg-cures are so popular in the Midwest, as it's the only way to utilize the natural bait. This is the first of five single-egg cures, and one Keene has applied for years.

He insists loose eggs are a must, as scraping them from immature skeins doesn't yield the quality product you are trying to attain. When a hen is caught, remove the eggs as soon as possible and place in a cooler. For best results, Keene recommends starting this cure within 24 hours of a fish being caught.

Once home, mix the ingredients in a container of water until they fully dissolve. Before combining

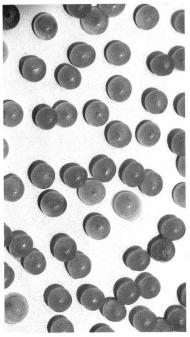

On his single-egg cure, Keene suggests starting with loose, ripe single eggs.

your eggs with the solution, place them in a strainer and run cold tap water over them. This washes any blood, slime, or bacteria from the eggs and hardens them up. With the excess water drained from them, dump the eggs into a clean jar.

Keene likes a glass jar, filing it to within an inch of the top. Do not pack the eggs down. The size jar(s) you use depends on the quantity of eggs you're curing. With the eggs in the jar, pour in enough solution to cover all the eggs. Seal the jar, placing it in a cool place, such as a basement. Keene cautions against letting direct sunlight come in contact with the eggs, for fear of spoiling.

Once a day during the next three or four days, turn the jar over to allow the ingredients to precipitate through and soak into the eggs. The boric acid acts to set the eggs up, while the sulfate preserves them. "The final product is amazingly strong and nearly bounces like a superball," advises Keene.

The eggs from this cure last indefinitely, and there is no need to freeze or refrigerate. Tied in different colored spawn bags, these eggs can be deadly.

The finished product is incredibly durable and bounces off the floor like a rubber ball.

Fishing and Curing Single Eggs

Though curing single eggs to be used in roe bags is a budding concept among many Pacific Northwest anglers, it's a practice commonly applied in Midwest and East Coast states. For Westerners, utilizing this technique can be especially effective when hens with ripe oversized eggs are taken. On more than one occasion I've landed, or seen caught, hens nearing the spawning stage, where the eggs spewed from them upon being lifted into the boat. Many West Coast anglers would discard those eggs, but to people who routinely catch such fish, curing loose eggs and tying them in roe bags is a unique way of utilizing one of nature's baits. It also adds to your egg arsenal which can be valuable when searching for variations to fool fish, or when you're in need of enhancing a dwindling egg supply.

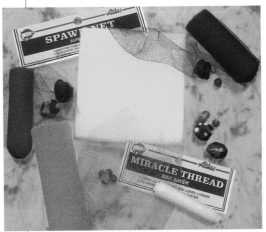

Preparing a variety of roe bags, in both size and color, is important in determining what fish like.

An estimated 90% of the roe fishing done in Wisconsin, Michigan, and New York is devoted to spawn sacks. The purpose of curing eggs in this manner is to attain a tough, realistic-looking bait that fishes well under various water conditions. Also, many of the salmon and steelhead in these waters are hatchery stock and harvested at times of the year when their eggs are fully mature, making it difficult to cure eggs in clusters.

One advantage to placing eggs in roe bags is that it prevents trout from stripping them while you're trying to get down to where the salmon and steelhead lay. Additionally, drifted in shallow, clear waters on lightweight line – often without any weight – roe bags create one of the more realistic presentations egg fishermen can offer. Curing the eggs is one step, bagging them is another.

Once the eggs are cured, place your desired quantity atop a square of Spawn Net. These nettings come in a variety of colors. Some anglers who want a color not available on the commercial market will purchase mesh, nylon fabric, or women's scarves in colors ranging from rich purple to neon pink.

The size of bait you fish will be determined by river levels, water clarity, and turbidity. Typically, the clearer and slower the stream flow, the smaller the bait so as not to risk spooking fish. If you want the bait to float higher, add styrofoam floater beads. Pick up the corners of the Spawn Net, bring them together so the net is taut against the eggs, and make three wraps with Magic Thread. Pull the thread tight and make three more wraps. This specialty thread is self-binding and is quick and easy to work with. When the wrapping is complete, simply trim the edges of the netting and thread and you have a nice, bait-sized bundle of eggs ready to fish. This process needs to be completed before leaving home, where many baits can be prepared, thereby optimizing your fishing time when on the river.

Once in the roe bag, scents and oils can be applied. "This is something that's becoming more and more popular, and proving very effective," attests Tom Vander Mause, President of Atlas-Mike's Bait Incorporated. "We've been supplying products to salmon, trout, and steelhead anglers for over 65 years, and the scents and oils end of things have really taken off." Depending on the kinds of scent being use (water base or oil base), they can be added to the eggs during the curing process, once the eggs have set up or when you're on the river.

Atlas' Spawn Net components are among the most popular in the industry, and are easy to work with.

There are two-ways to attach roe bags to your hook: through an egg loop or threaded directly on to the hook. Egg loops are tied on the back of the shank, cinched up snug below the eye, holding the eggs in place. This style of hookup offers the best opportunity to attach colored yarn, either on the leader, above the eye of the hook, or tied within the loop itself. The idea is to drape the yarn over the eggs, adding color. This is ideal in murky or fast-moving water, where sight cues will trigger a bite.

The most popular hookup method is running the point of the hook

Spawn nets can be attached to the hook in various ways.

through the bag, either directly beneath the knot or through the middle. If threading your hook through the middle of the sack, be careful not to puncture any eggs. When threading the hook below the knot in the sack, it will dangle from the bottom of the hook. These techniques are especially effective when fishing clear water with a low flow-volume. In extremely low, clear water, a single egg can be placed in a sack and the hook inserted right below the knot.

With some of the "how-to" of roe-sack fishing fresh in our mind, let's look at some cures that help make this method so effective. Following is a cure that's been time-tested and, most importantly, catches fish.

INGREDIENTS
- Rock salt
- Water

British Columbia guide, David Murphy, of Murphy's Sportfishing, spends 250 days a year fishing B.C. waters, where he's been guiding the past 16 years for salmon, steelhead, and halibut. Murphy has appeared on several television shows and has been instrumental in crafting instructional videos on sport fishing.

Since the early 1990s, Murphy has been curing single eggs for use in roe bags. Murphy uses a salt brine that he claims makes the eggs turn out like marbles.

Start by gently removing the single eggs from a skein. If the skeins are mature, oftentimes you can shake the cells free. If the skeins are young, carefully remove the eggs so as not to damage them. Murphy suggests going to a nearby hatchery during spawning season and collecting eggs that have been discarded or that are lying around and will not be used. He points out that these plump, mature eggs are best for this particular cure.

The single eggs will be added to a 100% salt solution, which is obtained by dumping a cup of rock salt into a strainer, then slowly pouring water over it, allowing it to precipitate into a jar. This jar will serve as the curing vat.

Place the eggs in the salt brine and let sit. After 24 hours, they are firm and ready to fish. "I've left eggs refrigerated in the brine for three weeks and they looked and fished very well," comments Murphy. He adds that you can also freeze these eggs by dumping them, brine and all, into plastic containers or sturdy Ziploc bags. He cautions that in a freezer, the eggs will likely shrivel and lose their color, turning white, but says once they thaw they reabsorb water and regain their color.

Because of the density of these eggs, Murphy uses foam balls to keep the roe bags afloat. "These are the least buoyant of the naturally-cured eggs and you have to lift them up off the bottom, where fish can see them," adds Murphy.

Sadly, Murphy is becoming surrounded by Canadian rivers closed to roe fishing, but he does remarkably well on streams still open to natural bait. From fast waters that test the stability of eggs, to low, transparent streams requiring a natural look, this is one of Murphy's preferred cures. He's cured all species of salmon and steelhead eggs applying this method and is happy with the results...so are his clients.

David Murphy uses a 100% salt solution to firm his single eggs.

Single-Egg Variations

INGREDIENTS

- 1 cup loose eggs
- 1/4 cup noniodized salt
- 1/4 cup white sugar
- 1 cup water

Immediately upon catching a fish, Brian Kelly places the single eggs into a nylon stocking and places them in the river. This quickly firms the eggs.

The following recipes come from Brian Kelly who lives outside of Detroit, Michigan. Brian and his buddy Wayne "Yogi" Ruston have tried about every cure imaginable, but consider these two among the best. Eggs from these cures have been tested on nearly every river and stream in Michigan, proving very effective.

For the first cure, begin by washing a cup of loose eggs in cold water. This is best done immediately after catching a ripe salmon whose eggs are mature and loose. As soon as she expires, remove the eggs and place them in a sock or nylon stocking, then submerge the eggs in a section of running water for 15-30 minutes. "Allowing the water to wash over the eggs will firm them up. We judge how firm the eggs are by feel. If they are tough to bust by squeezing between thumb and forefinger, you know they're ready. The waters in this section of the country are frigid, and the cold-water wash works well in setting up the eggs," comments Kelly.

Once home, mix the salt and sugar into one cup of water until fully dissolved. Then add one cup of loose eggs to the brine. The eggs will float in the beginning stages of the curing process. Cover the container with a lid or plastic wrap and store overnight – or for about six to eight hours – in the refrigerator. When the eggs start increasing their density and sinking to the bottom of the jar, you know they are done. "At this point, the eggs are ready to fish and will be hard as rubber balls, making them very durable," points out Kelly.

In this cure, the salt acts as a hardener while the sugar adds a bit of flavor and gives texture to the membrane.

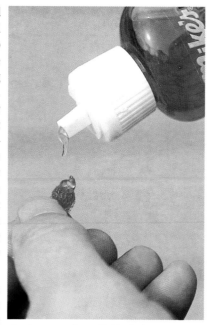

Scents can even be applied to single eggs.

At this stage, Kelly ties up several roe bags to last a few fishing trips and places them in brine in the refrigerator. For long-term storage, put the brine and eggs in canning jars and stick in the freezer. The salt content is so high, the water and eggs won't freeze. You can freeze and thaw this cure as much as you'd like and the eggs seem to last forever. He's fished with eggs from this cure that have been frozen for five years and they looked and fished wonderfully.

When on the river, scents can be added to the egg sacks to enhance the presentation. Kelly has had good luck using Pro-Cure scents and oils. The roe bags can also be soaked in these scents a day or so prior to fishing, allowing them to marinate.

INGREDIENTS

- 1 skein of eggs
- Pro-Cure Bait Cure (natural)
- Noniodized salt

This is a fast-reacting cure that Kelly says will produce fishable eggs in a couple hours. Note that it's not a hard egg cure, but one that's worked well for he and Yogi in extremely cold waters, where fish tend to mouth baits instead of aggressively attacking them.

The skeins used in this cure are typically younger than those used in the above cure, and therefore more durable to work with. Take a spoon and remove the eggs from the skein, being careful not to rupture them in the process. Spread the eggs out on a white paper towel and sprinkle with white Pro-Cure Bait Cure until they have a light layer of powder on them. Be careful not to add too much Pro-Cure, which will burn the eggs.

Using rubber gloves, gently roll the eggs around until each is completely covered in Pro-Cure. Once covered in the powdered cure, sprinkle salt over all of the eggs to firm them up. Place the eggs in the refrigerator and let sit for two hours. At this point they are ready to fish or be stored.

The eggs can be placed in jars and put in the freezer where they will keep for up to a year. Since this cure does not refreeze well, Kelly likes putting the eggs in small, baby-food size jars, about what you'd use in one day of fishing.

If the eggs are not loose, Kelly has had good luck scooping them from skeins.

The finished product from this cure has a natural look, much like an uncured egg. "This cure is dynamite on spooky fish as they seem to hang on to it longer," claims Kelly. Kelly and Yogi have used this cure extensively throughout many Midwestern drainages and feel confident it will work in streams wherever steelhead and trout are found.

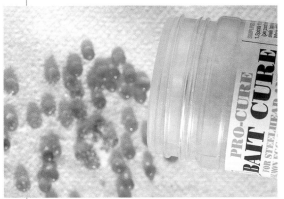

Kelly prefers applying Pro-Cure Bait Cure to his single eggs.

Formaldehyde & Borax

INGREDIENTS
- 1 cup loose eggs
- 2 pints water
- 4 tablespoons formaldehyde
- 1/2 cup brown sugar

The two recipes in this chapter come from Ron Little of Windsor, Ontario. Ron's been tinkering with egg cures for the past quarter-century and takes it seriously. He's not about to give in to fishing with floats, and is determined to find prime cures that allow him to continue rolling eggs along the bottom, no matter what the water conditions. Ron was gracious enough to share his two favorite single-egg cures, and they are surprisingly simple.

Ron Little's favorite cure calls for interesting ingredients.

The first begins by putting two pints of cool water into a glass jar. Add the formaldehyde and brown sugar to the jar and mix thoroughly. Once the brown sugar has dissolved, add the cup of loose eggs and let stand for 30 minutes. After this time, drain the excess water and tie the eggs in roe sacks; they are ready to fish.

For long-term storage, put the roe bags in small plastic containers and place in the refrigerator. The shelf life of eggs cured in this brine will last for three weeks in the refrigerator. If placed in the freezer, they can keep for five to six years. Ron will freeze them in either glass jars or Ziploc bags.

Whichever you use, be sure the air is removed from the containers to ensure longer keeping. If freezing in baggies, roll up the bags to force out the air, then seal. In glass jars, toss a piece of burning wax paper inside before securing the lid. Snug the lid down with the flame still burning; this will use up all the oxygen in the jar.

This is a unique recipe in that formaldehyde is utilized. Formaldehyde is a preservative that will also toughen the eggs. The brown sugar adds color to the eggs, highlighting yellows and brightening up the end product. The finished eggs will come out tough, literally capable of bouncing off the kitchen floor. Little

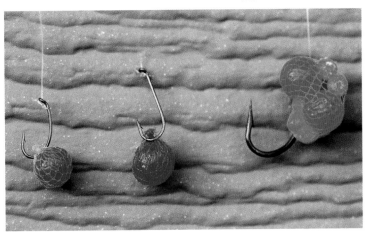

Putting up single eggs in a variety of colored bags can improve success.

In low, clear streams, size 16 and 14 hooks, on up to size 1s, can be effective on single egg setups.

cautions against producing too firm an egg, for fear of turning the fish off should they mouth it. "I like an egg that will break when firmly squeezed between my fingers. I feel it's a more realistic presentation," adds Little.

Formaldehyde can be challenging to find, with scientific supply companies being the best bet. Be sure to wear gloves when handling this chemical and take extra measures not to inhale the fumes.

INGREDIENTS
• Borax

Eggs placed in cold water turn surprisingly white, especially when compared to fresh, untouched eggs.

Many of the anglers I've spoken with about single-egg cures stick with the old standby: borax. Borax cures are easy to work with, produce very real-looking eggs, protect against freezer burn and preserve well. This is a recipe Ron keeps coming back to.

This cure begins when you're on the river. As soon as a mature hen is taken, quickly remove the loose salmon or steelhead eggs and place in a small, leakproof plastic bag that can be tied at the top. Put enough river water in the bag to cover all of the eggs, then tie it off in a tree. Little warns, "In really cold water, some of the eggs will turn white and the eye of the egg may even pop up, but that's okay, they'll regain their color later."

After two hours, punch a few small holes in the bottom of the bag to fully drain the water. Remove the eggs from the bag and spread them out on a paper towel to air-dry. "Be careful on hot days, you don't want the eggs dried to the point they are hard and useless," cautions Little. Under most conditions, about 30 minutes of drying time is about right. Once dry to the touch — where they are rubbery feeling — transfer the eggs to another, clean paper towel and cover in borax. Make certain all parts of the eggs are covered in borax, you may need to roll them around to achieve full coverage.

If you'll be fishing within the next few days, simply place the eggs in a glass jar and put in the refrigerator. The remainder of the eggs can be placed in jars and frozen. Eggs cured in this way can last several years in the freezer. When transferring from the freezer to spawn bags, it takes only 30 minutes for these eggs to thaw. The borax which is on the eggs will be whisked away by the water on the first cast.

Little has used these cures to take salmon, trout, and steelhead throughout the Great Lakes region. He's also used them in British Columbia with good success. Anglers hitting clear, low-water streams will want to give these cures a try.

Sardine Wrap Cure

INGREDIENTS
- Dr. Juice (Salmon Scent)
- Borax

A scent that has proven effective in eggs, on flies, and with sardines, is Dr. Juice, in Salmon Scent. This is a product made to mimic fear pheromones released by baitfish, and can be very effective.

I've heard of guys pulling into holes on the river choked with drift boats, where no one had touched a fish all day. They started fishing with Dr. Juice on their baits and triggered a bite. Not only did they catch fish, but nearly everyone in their direct vicinity caught fish.

Veteran guide, Jason Dunkin, was turned on to Dr. Juice many years ago. Dunkin was fishing fall chinook in a small, shallow, crystal-clear coastal stream. There were more than twenty anglers fishing the hole Dunkin wanted to work. Rigging his fly setup, he was discouraged to hear no one had caught a fish all morning. The water was so clear everyone could see the chinook cruising around and schooling in ideal pools, but the fish would not bite.

Dunkin tried an egg imitation with no luck. Then he applied a drop of Dr. Juice to his pattern. He and his buddy nailed three kings in a row, and that was only the beginning. Not only did it set off a feeding frenzy in the hole they fished, but anglers well down stream started catching fish. In a very short span of time, several anglers caught fish, and if you think about why this happened, it makes sense.

In the low-water conditions, as soon as the fear pheromone hit the water, it set off a chain reaction in the salmon – to feed on anything in their path, much like they do in the ocean when feeding on schooling baitfish. This got Dunkin thinking. If it works on artificial flies, it should work on egg cures.

The oil worked on egg cures, too, though not to the extent Dunkin claims other oils do on some of his more secretive egg-curing recipes. With that mind, Dunkin was kind enough to disclose his favorite sardine cure.

Dunkin guides in both Oregon and Alaska, and has taken his share of trophy salmon and steelhead in both states. Next to his eggs, Dunkin ranks his wrapped sardines among his most important weapons.

Start with frozen sardines, removing them from the freezer the night before you intend to fish. When they are about half-thawed, carefully fillet them out, trying to maintain a long, slender cut. It's much easier cutting fillets off a half-frozen fish versus a soft, slimy one. When all your fillets are cut, add a few drops of Dr. Juice Salmon Scent to each fillet and let sit for 20 minutes. You can also submerge the fillets in Dr. Juice, but be sure to strain the oil from the baits.

Next, place some borax in a Ziploc bag and add the fillets. Gently shake the bag to disperse the borax thoroughly around the fillets. Let them set in the borax overnight to firm up. This process saves time and eliminates a mess when compared to cutting the fillets in the boat. It also makes handling the baits a much cleaner affair, because you're touching only the dried, firm, borax-treated fillet, not the oily, soft fish we've all struggled with. This also makes wrapping the fillets around your plug very easy.

One of the aspects that turns people off to herring, sardines, or anchovies for bait, is that they turn soft very rapidly. This can result in a short fishing life for your baits. Treating the fillets in borax increases the baits longevity by at least three times, Dunkin has determined. And it works on cohos as well as kings.

"I prefer using sardines over herring and anchovies, for they have the best oil and work better for me under a Kwikfish," offers Dunkin. "I also like the longest fillet I can slice. The longer the bait, the more surface area you have on which to put your scents, and the more scent you have, the better

your odds of catching fish. I like a piece of fillet that's long, but not so long as to interfere with the action of my plug. I tediously cut each fillet, making sure it's streamlined. The more angular cuts you have, the more it throws off a plug's action. Take time to make precision cuts and clean up any rough edges that may exist," advises Dunkin.

Dunkin removes the front hook from his Kwikfish and drops the trailing hook back. He believes this has dramatically increased his bite-to-hook ratio.

Typically, K14, K15 and K16 sized Kwikfish are used to wrap fillets on. Dunkin prefers cutting lengths of fillets that will cover 2/3 of the plug's length. Many people use only a tiny chunk, tying it to the plug. The smaller the bait, the less scent enters the water, so try and master the skill of crafting long, aerodynamic fillets. The ultimate goal is to achieve a long bait that will fit snug on the plug, without having to tune it.

His plug setup is also unique, and one that's increased his bite-to-hook-ratio by 75%. Dunkin often removes the front hook from his Kwikfish, simply because it makes it easier to wrap the fillet onto the plug. It also ensures you don't have two hooks fighting against one another once a fish is hooked. Dunkin then removes the back hook, inserts an O-ring into the back eye of the plug, then threads a barrel swivel through the O-ring. On the opposite end of the barrel swivel he slips on another O-ring, then slides his

Jason Dunkin's large frame does not do this 65-pound Kenai king justice.

hook into that O-ring. This drops the trailing hook a considerable distance, meaning the fish hits the stinger right off, rather than mouthing the plug and not getting hooked.

Born and raised in Dallas, Oregon, Dunkin began fishing at the age of six. He now guides year-round, from Alaska to Oregon. He spends a lot of his time on two of the world's most important fisheries: the Columbia and Kenai.

One day last spring on the Columbia, three of Dunkin's clients landed 19 kings by 11:00 a.m. But that's not all he fishes. Dunkin hits the Nestucca, Trask, and Tillamook drainages as well as the Rogue and Siletz when he needs to. He'll go wherever he has to to catch fish, and that persistence is what makes him such a successful guide. In spring, Dunkin concentrates on chinook in Oregon, then heads to Alaska in the summer.

He's been guiding on the Kenai and Kasilof rivers since the early '90s. Once that wraps up in early August, Dunkin is back in Oregon, hitting fall chinook, silvers, and preparing for winter steelhead.

Conclusion

In the Introduction, I mentioned several guides are utilizing many of the prepackaged, commercial cures now on the market. Recreational fishermen are doing the same thing, for the simple reason of convenience.

I've personally tested many of the packaged cures currently on the market and was impressed, overall, by the end results. Pictured within this

chapter are several of these cures, and the eggs which came from them. Be it colored borax or high-chemical cures, there are several variations available.

Don't neglect dyes. There are some incredible dyes on the market. Be it liquid or powder form, dyes are being used more and

Quick Cure has four variations of egg cures, all of which are proven and produce quality eggs.

Beau Mac's Pro Glow Egg Cure and the eggs cured in each.

more by anglers. Not only are dyes useful in giving eggs a desired color during the initial curing phase, they are a good way to add color to milked-out eggs, something any angler whose egg supply has dwindled can appreciate as he fishes each bait until it's milked to the point of being ivory in color.

Beau Mac makes quality egg cures and arguably the best dyes on the market.

Siberian Egg Cure is a cure that shouldn't be overlooked.

Mr. Shur-Cure is popular among many anglers.

Atlas Shake "N" cure is easy to work with and yields good-colored eggs.

The information offered in this book has presented many facets in egg curing for you to explore. Only by expanding our mindset and exploring new, unfamiliar approaches, can we fully realize what it takes to increase our catch.

On a recent trip down the river, Dad and I were loading the riverboat onto the trailer. I began snapping pictures of eggs from the day's catch. "Whatchya up to, young man?" asked an elderly gentleman standing on the bank. "Getting some shots for a book I'm writing on egg cures. Have anything you'd like to share?" I replied.

The gentleman went on to talk about how he's used the same cure for nearly half a century, and was curious as to why a book on egg cures would be of interest. "My egg cure has worked fine for me, why would I want to change?" he inquired.

That's the point of this book. If you limit yourself to only one egg cure, how do you know it worked to its full capacity?

Pro-Cure has two borax cures. For dyed borax cures, they produce good-colored eggs steelheaders find very effective.

Alaskan Premier Bait is a borax cure many anglers like, especially when fishing for steelhead.

There's nothing by which to compare it to, thus, no basis upon which to draw any valid conclusion.

We've all come off the river pumped up about hooking a good number of fish, feeling good about how effective our cure was, only to run across another angler who outfished us. At the time, your mindset may have been, "there's no other cure as effective as this one." Who is to say another cure may not have produced even more fish. Or better yet, trying a different cure when the bite may have slowed, may have turned them on.

Both of these cured baits sat side-by-side in a stream for 15 minutes. The one on the right then had Beau Mac's Instant Bait Coloring applied to it.

I'm not asking you to sacrifice your favorite cure, I would never do that myself. I have carried my most coveted eggs with me every time I've gone out for the past 30 years, but I like having two or three other options from which to choose, when my eggs aren't producing. By opening your mind to unfamiliar aspects of our sport, only then can you begin to fathom the untapped potential which exists.

That's the beauty of egg cures.

Pro Glow Bait Coloring yields vibrant eggs.   *Smelly Jelly scent can be applied to any eggs.*

If you're not into curing and bagging your own single eggs, Atlas sells several varieties.

About the Author

Scott Haugen was born and raised on Oregon's McKenzie River. He grew up fishing, hunting and trapping throughout the Willamette Valley and parts of Oregon. By age four he was accompanying his father and grandfather on the river in search of salmon and steelhead.

With a master's degree in education, Scott and his wife Tiffany, spent several years in Alaska's Arctic, teaching in some of the world's most remote Eskimo villages. From there, the Haugens relocated to Sumatra, Indonesia.

Haugen's passion for the outdoors has taken him around the world. The author of hundreds of articles appearing in more than 40 magazines, Haugen has also written books on hunting and fishing.

The Haugens currently live in Oregon where they pursue full-time writing careers and spend time with their two young sons. Prime fishing is only minutes from their doorstep.

Resources

SCOTT AMERMAN
AMERMAN'S EGGS

P.O. Box 228
Hebo, OR 97122
(503) 392-9468
(503) 392-9450
e-mail:
amerman@oregoncoast.com
www.ifish.net/amer.html

ATLAS-MIKE'S BAIT, INC.
P.O. Box 608
Fort Atkinson, WI 53538
(920) 563-2046

BEAU MAC ENTERPRISES
PRO-GLOW PRODUCTS
3280 B St. N.W. #V
Auburn, WA 98001
(253) 939-8607

MIKE BOGUE
MIKE BOGUE'S GUIDE SERVICE
5887 Live Oak Lane
Redding, CA 96001
(530) 246-8457
e-mail: mike@mikebogue.com
www.mikebogue.com

CATCHER COMPANY
(Smelly Jelly)
5285 N.E. Elam Young Pkwy
Suite B700
Hillsboro, OR 97124
(503) 648-2643

CURE-RITE PRODUCTS
P.O. Box 681
Tillamook, OR 97141
(503) 842-5550

JASON DUNKIN
SLAM DUNKIN GUIDE SERVICE
(503) 623-6965
e-mail:
dunkin@slamdunkin.com
www.slamdunkin.com

GAMAKATSU USA, INC.
WESTERN U.S:
P.O. Box 1797
Tacoma, WA 98401

EASTERN U.S:
3900 Kennesaw 75 Pkwy.
Suite 140
Kennesaw, GA 30144

BRETT GESH
ALASKAN BITE FINDERS
P.O. Box 3093
Soldotna, AK 99669
(907) 223-8704
e-mail:
bitefinders@yahoo.com

BRUCE GIPPLE
2210 W. Main St.
#107-312
Battle Ground, WA 98604
(360) 887-3676
e-mail: hwest@teleport.com
www.horizonwestguides.com

LUHR-JENSEN & SONS, INC.
P.O. Box 297
Hood River, OR 97031
(541) 386-3811
www.luhrjensen.com

DAVID MURPHY
MURPHY'S SPORTFISHING
British Columbia
e-mail: murphy@island.net
www.murphysportfishing.com
1-877-218-6600
(250) 723-2772

PAUTZKE'S BAIT CO., INC.
P.O. Box 36
Ellensburg, WA 98926

PRO-CURE BAIT SCENTS
P.O. Box 7077
2990 Portland Road NE
Salem, OR 97303
1-800-776-2873
www.pro-cure.com

MR. SHUR-CURE
P. O. Box 253
Tillamook, OR 97141

SPRINGFIELD SCIENTIFIC, INC.
2600 Main Street #A
Springfield, OR 97477
1-800-344-2047
www.springfieldsci.com

BRET STUART
24/7 GUIDE SERVICE
P.O. Box 125
Thurston, OR 97482
1-888-761-5203
(541) 988-3828
e-mail: fishnfamily@juno.com
www.fish24-7.com

T-N-T EGG CURE
Midway Sports Center
4432 Hwy. 20
Sweet Home, OR 97386
1-888-223-1331
(541) 367-4128
e-mail: tnt@peak.org
www.midwaysportscenter.com

CHRIS VERTOPOULOS
NORTHWEST ANGLING
EXPERIENCE
P.O. Box 1120
Tillamook, OR, 97141
(503) 815-2822
(503) 335-3849 (voicemail)

WORDEN'S LURES/
YAKIMA BAIT CO.
P.O. Box 310
Granger, WA 98932
(509) 854-1311
www.yakimabait.com

Index